T0145434

BIG EYES

Published by Advantage, Charleston, South Carolina.
Member of Advantage Media Group.

ADVANTAGE is a registered trademark and the Advantage colophon is a trademark of Advantage Media Group, Inc.

Printed in the United States of America.

ISBN: 978-1-59932-084-7

BIG EYES

Big Eyedeas for
Achieving Optimum
SUCCESS
in Business and in Life

Daisy M. Saunders

Note from the Author

I acknowledge all writers I have quoted. An exhaustive search was done to determine whether previously published material included in this book required permission to reprint. If there has been an error, I apologize and a correction will be made in subsequent editions.

The following authors, their agents, and publishers have graciously granted permission to include the following:

Quote from pages 32-33 is from the book *Visionary Business*. Copyright 1995 by Marc Allen. Reprinted with permission of New World Library, Novato, California.

Paraphrased story on page 117 is taken with permission from *Think and Grow Rich – A Black Choice* by Napoleon Hill and Dennis Kimbro. Copyright 1991 by the Napoleon Hill Foundation.

Photo by Barbara Banks Photography, Sarasota, Florida

Dedication

Dedicated to all of the workshop and seminar participants I have had the pleasure of teaching and learning from over the past twenty-five years. You empowered me. You convinced me that I had a "gift" for making old information sound new.

Thank you for your support, encouragement, and love.

CONTENTS

Success is the progressive realization of predetermined, worthwhile goals.

\- Paul J. Meyer

To succeed, we must first believe that we can.

\- Michael Korda

Success often comes to those who have the aptitude to see way down the road.

\- J. Laing Burns, Jr.

Success doesn't come to you…you go to it.

\- Marva Collins

No one ever attains very eminent success by simply doing what is required of him; it is the amount and excellence of what is over and above the required that determines the greatness of ultimate distinction.

\- Charles Kendall Adams

Success is a journey, not a destination.

\- Ben Sweetland

In order to succeed, your desire for success should be greater than your fear of failure.

\- Bill Cosby

Vision is the art of seeing what is invisible to others.

- Jonathan Swift

They spoke as if she wasn't in the room, the old women did. "Something is wrong with her; her eyes are too big," they said. She just kept reading as if they weren't in the room. She knew, with that innate instinct bestowed upon every child, that although her eyes were big in size, they weren't talking about the size of her eyes but the size of her dreams. She also knew that the problem wasn't that her eyes were too big, but that theirs were too small. They were unable to see anything beyond the small world they inhabited.

She could see, even then, far beyond the tobacco fields of Quincy, Florida. Beyond the tobacco processing plant where, considered "slow", she was relegated to the easy jobs – jobs that gave her time to dream and read about the world in which she would someday make her mark.

Fast forward.

Today Daisy Saunders, the little girl with the big eyes, is a successful entrepreneur, motivational and inspirational speaker, trainer, life coach, real estate investor, and published author whose eyes have seen much of the world.

In *Big Eyes...Big Eyedeas for Achieving Optimum Success in Business and in Life* she shares it all. The complete recipe for achieving optimum success is here. All you have to do is envision the possibilities, take action, and claim what God has waiting for you.

Keith Harrell
Dr. Attitude
Author, *Attitude is Everything*

Success is a state of mind.
If you want success, start thinking of yourself as a success.

- Dr. Joyce Brothers

Success is possible. Everyone has the capacity to achieve optimum success. What is success and how is it achieved? Success is personal. It can't be specifically defined for the masses because it's subject to individual interpretation based on upbringing, past experiences, personal motivations, values, and goals. It means different things to different people.

For some, "success" is money, power, prominence, or importance. For others, it is excellence, meaningful relationships, purpose, or achieving specific goals. For example, to Keith Harrell, renowned motivational speaker and author of *Attitude Is Everything: Ten Life-Changing Steps to Turning Attitude Into Action*, success is "fulfilling God's purpose for your life." To Dale Carnegie, author of *How to Win Friends and Influence People,* success was achieving goals – getting what you want. To me, success is having the ability to give and live abundantly.

To achieve success, first you must know what success looks like to you. Does it look like fame, riches, distinction, meaningful relationships, or achieving goals? If you don't know what it looks like, it is difficult to achieve. For me, success started with a dream, and it looked like fortune, excellence, and service. Fortune, because I wanted to have the experiences and the lifestyle I dreamed of and read about while growing up in Quincy, Florida. Excellence, because it was instilled in us that good was not enough, that we had to be better than good in order to succeed. And service, because we were indoctrinated with the idea that "from those to whom much is given, much is expected."

Second, to achieve success you must "intend" to be successful. In other words, you must make a conscious effort to be successful, be committed to success, and have a hunger and desire to "have more," "be more," and "do more." Some people are fortunate enough to be born into successful families and may have an edge. Most people must orchestrate their own success.

Big Eyes...Big Eyedeas for Achieving Optimum Success in Business and in Life is more than the title of this book. It is my charge to you to always strive for optimum success each and every day – in business and in life.

Big Eyes...Big Eyedeas for Achieving Optimum Success in Business and in Life is designed to give you the motivation you need to achieve success in your life and career, get healthier, build relationships that work, and find focus, peace of mind, and a sense of purpose – all of the things necessary to live abundantly and joyfully. The book not only tells you what to do to achieve optimum success, it goes much further and explains how. It explores and provides you with ten simple yet profound, easy-to-implement "how-to" strategies:

- Examine Your Picture: Widen Your Eyes

- Adjust Your Picture: For Your Big Eyes Only

- Have a Clear Vision: See the Possibilities with Big Eyes

- Set Goals: Keep Your Big Eyes Clear

- Focus: Keep Your Big Eyes on the Prize

- Build Relationships: Surround Yourself with Big-Eyed People

- Be Positive: Keep Your Big Eyes Bright

- Practice Self-Care: To Thine Own Big Eyes Be Good

- Mind Your Money: Open Your Big Eyes to Wealthfulness

- Give Back: Shine Your Big Eyes on Others

Your "how" will be revealed to you as you read each chapter and make your notes on the workbook pages throughout the book and at the end of the book.

I know these strategies work because they worked for me. They helped me to move from that little insecure girl – the dreamer with the big eyes, one of nine children born to sharecroppers – to entrepreneur, motivational and inspirational speaker, trainer, life coach, real estate investor, and published author. They have also worked in the lives of many of my family members, friends, associates, and students. And I am confident they will work for you – if you work them.

My goal is for you to fully realize that optimum success isn't a rare gift available only to a few. It is a gift that's within everyone's capacity to achieve. I want you to begin, today, envisioning all of the possibilities that are in store for you-- in business and in life.

Are you ready to awaken your success gene? Then let's get started!

Think on This: What is success and how do you achieve it?

Act on This: In the space below or on a separate sheet of paper, write your personal definition of success. In other words, what does success look like to you? Does it look like riches, fame, meaningful relationships, self-satisfaction, etc.? Be as specific as possible. You may wish to return to this description often as you progress through this book.

Chapter 1

EXAMINE YOUR PICTURE

Widen Your Eyes

A strong, positive self-image is the best possible
preparation for success.
- Dr. Joyce Brothers

To start and stay on the path that leads you to optimum success, you must first open your eyes to examine yourself – to see what you believe about yourself and why. In other words, you must look at your mental picture – your self-image.

We cannot deny the power of an image. Image is two-sided. There is the internal, or self-image, which is the way we perceive ourselves. And there is the external image, the way others perceive us. Both are important. The focus in this chapter, however, is on the internal or self-image.

The picture we have of ourselves is much more important than the picture others have of us. The image we have of ourselves contributes to, and helps form, the image that others have of us. When we think highly of ourselves, it's reflected in our behavior, our thoughts, and our actions. I have discovered that people will treat us the way they see us. The way they see us is often similar to the way we see ourselves.

If we project an image of strength and confidence, of someone who is worthy of happiness, health, and wealth, people will associate those qualities and characteristics with us. On the other hand, if we project weakness and insecurity, that's how others will perceive us.

A few years ago, I met a successful mortgage broker who had been in the business since his early twenties. By age thirty-eight, he had made a name for himself and was doing quite well financially.

Curious, I asked what had contributed to his success at such an early age. Without hesitation, he replied: "I work hard and I'm real smart." I thought to myself, *Here's a young man with big eyes and big eyedeas.*

He went on to say that he had gotten into the mortgage business because he thought he could make a lot of money, and he felt this way because he noticed that most real estate agents were women. He was not only hardworking and smart, but good looking, and he sensed that he could get these agents to refer customers to him. Today his company writes 20% or more of the mortgages written in the area where he does business.

His image of himself as someone who is intelligent, confident, attractive, and successful radiates outward. The people he does business with perceive him in much the same way he perceives himself. He has learned and uses the power of a positive self-image to help him realize his dreams of success. By his beliefs about himself, he is creating a self-fulfilling path to optimum success.

> **The mental picture we paint for and of ourselves impacts virtually everything we do, or will ever attempt to do.**

Our self-image affects every aspect of our lives – our performance, our ability to learn and earn, our attitudes and beliefs, our choices of friends, the amount of risk we are willing to take in pursuit of our dreams, and even our career choices. The mental picture we paint for and of ourselves impacts virtually everything we do, or will ever attempt to do. It's not our gender, race, upbringing, childhood experiences, parents, siblings, spouses, significant others, or educational background that stand in the way of our success. It's the mental picture we carry around with us each and every day of our lives.

Make no mistake: numerous people at various stages of our lives have impacted the perception we have of ourselves, both positively and negatively, intentionally and unintentionally, and in verbal and nonverbal ways. The picture of ourselves that we carry around today started to gel in early childhood. So clearly, those people were influential in the formation of our self-image.

Way back then, unaware of the power we possessed, we allowed everyone and everything to help shape our self-image. Now, however, we realize that not only can we delete the negative images, we can stop, or at least severely limit, the ability of people and situations to negatively affect our self-image. By learning to bring the picture more into focus and eliminate the negative background, we can change the course of our lives.

Like most of us, my picture started to form early. I can think of many positive experiences that helped me create the mental picture I carry of myself to this day. They include strong and encouraging words from my mother, some of my teachers, and a neighbor who took a special interest in me, encouraging me and even supporting me financially during my first year of college.

I can also think of some not-so-positive experiences that were a part of the picture.

It's funny how the not-so-positives are the ones we remember the most. These are also the ones that, unfortunately, can have the greatest impact on our lives.

Two experiences in particular stand out in my mind. The first was my childhood, growing up in a small tobacco town in the Florida Panhandle. The second happened in college, during a speech class.

I grew up in the country, where there were dirt roads and outhouses. My mother was a domestic worker and my father worked in the fields. The major industry at that time in my hometown of Quincy, Florida, was tobacco. By today's standards we would be considered poor. Of course at that time we didn't consider ourselves poor because we were homeowners. We always had clothes to wear, we went to school, and we had plenty of good food to eat. We grew most of our food, and my mother made most of our clothes.

All the children from the "country"– the children of domestic workers, day laborers, and field hands – worked in tobacco.

So you guessed it. I was one of the tobacco workers.

You could tell who we were because when we returned to school after summer vacations (never a vacation to us) the tips of our fingers would be black from tobacco juice. This was quite embarrassing because it announced to the world that we lived way out in the country, on a dirt road, and had an outhouse instead of an in-house bathroom. Although we didn't consider ourselves poor, our more fortunate classmates did. So we were sometimes teased or snubbed.

In addition to being a tobacco worker, I was also teased about my looks. I wasn't considered a knock-out – skinny, bowlegs, and very big eyes. Over forty years ago these were not features that landed you a place in the "good looking" category. In the early sixties, voluptuous was in; skinny was out. And big eyes and bowlegs didn't get you a date to the prom. Often I was called Popeye – though my oldest brother lovingly referred to me as Olive Oyl. Imagine what that did to my self-image.

The second experience happened during my sophomore year of college. In high school I excelled at many things, especially acting and speaking. I was often told that I had the "gift of gab." I was even on the speaker's circuit in my little hometown of Quincy. Whenever there was a need for a youth day speaker at my church or a role available in a school or church play, I had little competition. The picture I carried of myself was of someone who was a talented and sought-after public speaker. So it was only natural that I was eager to further develop my speaking skills. In my second year of college, I enrolled in a speech class. Each week we were required to make a three-to five-minute speech. Confident in my speaking abilities, I was always the first person to volunteer to deliver my speech.

After the third or fourth session, the instructor asked me to stay after class. I just knew that he was going to compliment me on my speaking ability. Boy, was I in for a surprise! Not only did he make fun of the way I spoke, he laughingly said that I sounded like "poor trash from East Texas." I was crushed! From that day on I never volunteered to make a speech and I became overly conscious of my southern accent, my sometimes high-pitched voice, and my pronunciation of certain words.

That one conversation, those thoughtless and cruel words, and the way they were delivered had, in an instant, changed the picture I had of myself from something bright and optimistic to something dark and fearful.

Later I briefly entertained the thought of going to law school, but I quickly discarded that idea. I asked myself, *What if, in the courtroom, they laugh at the way I speak?*

It's amazing how an off-the-cuff remark can change the course of a life. I once read a story about a young gymnast, an Olympic hopeful, who overheard a judge refer to her as fat. The comment so impacted the girl that she developed anorexia and eventually starved herself to death.

While I don't believe that my speech instructor's intentions were to be cruel or to destroy my self-image, the damage was done nonetheless. In his own way, I think that he was just having fun with me. This may even have been an awkward attempt to give some guidance. But unintended or not, those words said in a joking manner had a tremendous impact on my beliefs about myself.

Although I have had a successful career as a speaker, seminar leader, and owner of a training company, there are still times when doubt tries to creep in and make me question my speaking abilities.

It took me years to get past that experience. Even now that teacher's words sometimes still haunt me. For example, when someone teases me about a word I may have mispronounced or makes a comment about my voice tone, I am transported back in time and become once again that young woman so full of expectation, until I hear my college speech instructor's voice and…

An even more poignant example of the impact words can have on you involves my niece, Kitrina. When Kitrina was about twelve years old, she wanted to be in the school band.

She went for band tryouts. After briefly observing her, the band teacher told her she didn't have any rhythm.

Disappointed, she left tryouts and never went back. When she told us what happened, she laughed (even though she was hurt), and we laughed. Since we didn't view this as a serious matter, we never gave it another thought nor, to my knowledge, was it ever discussed.

A few years later Kitrina came to spend the summer with me. One day she went with me to my aerobics class. I was stunned that she had no sense of rhythm and couldn't do the simplest dance steps. She was the only person in the class who couldn't keep step to the beat of the music or the moves.

I could see that the aerobics instructor was also surprised. He went over to work with her, one-on-one, but soon gave up after it became apparent that she heard a totally different beat.

Later when I asked her about it, she responded, "You know that I don't have rhythm." To this day, Kitrina's rhythm is off the beat. A thought that was planted over fifteen years ago still manifests today.

Sometimes teachers, parents, and significant and not-so-significant others say things, and these things have impact.

Perhaps you've had similar experiences – someone dashed your hopes, walked all over your dreams, muddied the picture you carry of yourself.

The good thing is that while we may never completely get over those down-to-the bone hurts, we can learn to pick up and dust off our dreams, to reawaken those faded self-images – to open our big eyes wide once again.

> Sometimes teachers, parents, and significant and not-so-significant others say things, and these things have impact.

In Chapter 2, I'll show you how to bring your picture back into focus – how to erase the negative tape and write a winning script for your life. I'll also share with you the personal script I used to bring my picture back into focus.

Key Points to Remember

The mental picture we have of ourselves is much more important than the picture others have of us. The mental picture we paint for and of ourselves impacts virtually everything we do or will ever attempt to do.

👁

Your image of yourself radiates outward. When we think highly of ourselves, it is reflected in our behavior, our thoughts, and our actions.

👁

The picture we carry around today started forming in early childhood.

👁

Unaware of the power we possessed, we allowed everyone and everything to help shape our self-image.

👁

An off-the-cuff remark – good or bad – can change the course of a life. So be careful what you say to others!

Think on This: What experiences helped to shape your self-image – positively or negatively?

Act on This: In the space below or on a separate sheet of paper, make some notes about your beliefs about yourself – positive, negative, and in-between. Don't judge them. Just list them. Add to your notes as memories surface or realizations occur. This is an essential step, but will also be an ongoing process.

Chapter 2

ADJUST YOUR PICTURE

For Your Big Eyes Only

Your self-image – who you think you are –
is literally a package you put together from how
others have seen and treated you and from your
conclusions as you compared yourself to others.

- Dorothy Corkille Briggs, Author, *Celebrate Your Self*

Our self image, strongly held, essentially
determines what we become.

- Maxwell Maltz, Author, *Psycho-Cybernetics*

Because a negative self-image is learned, it can be unlearned. But just as we don't learn it overnight, it won't disappear overnight. It's not a one-time shot. Like a bad habit, it's something we have to work on continuously to rid ourselves of. And yes, there is always the temptation to fall back on old, known, and familiar habits. In other words, we have to be vigilant not to let the negative self-image creep back in.

We all have our tapes – those messages that play in our heads. The scripts that play vary, depending on the circumstances we're dealing with. Some are positive, some are negative; some encourage us and some are self-defeating. The messages become such a big part of us that we don't even need to hit the play button for the tapes to start. And we become so accustomed to the tapes that often we are unaware they're even playing.

One of the best ways to unlearn a negative self-image is to erase the tape and create a new script. We need to widen our eyes to remind ourselves that we can be successful, not listen to the small voices telling us we can't be.

Creating a new tape in order to change your picture is much like eradicating weeds: you start at the root.

The following will help you recognize and unearth the roots of your negative tapes – how and when they developed, who was the bearer of the message, and why it took hold. Then you'll erase them and create a new tape.

BE AWARE OF PAST PROGRAMMING

It's important that we understand how we got where we are today and the experiences that influenced and helped to shape our lives.

Marc Allen, in his book *Visionary Business*, states:

It's important – in some cases critically important – to regularly examine our lives. The first thing to do is to take a look at our past and discover the important events and influences that have shaped our lives...Some of these shaping events have led to very good core beliefs – and those moments should be remembered, and those beliefs should be encouraged and supported. Those shaping moments that have had a negative impact on us need to be looked at, and we need to discover the negative core beliefs we formed as a result. This is the process of becoming conscious – becoming aware of the forces that drive us, and learning how to act on these forces, how to shape our destiny, how to become powerful, how to achieve what we want in life.

For me, the childhood teasing and the ridicule from my speech instructor were important events that shaped my beliefs about myself. We want to know the events (positives and negatives) that shaped our lives so we can make them work for, not against, us. We don't want to use these negative events and influences of the past as an excuse for not achieving what we want in life.

Today, so many people use their past wrongs or injustices to justify or excuse their behavior. Often I hear comments such as "I am insecure" or "I am a low achiever" or "I am .... (fill in the blank) because "I never knew my father" or "My mother abandoned me" or "I was placed in foster care" or "My father never told me he loved me." The list goes on and on.

These events can impact our lives. But they don't define our lives. At some point we "get over it" and say, "It happened.

I can't change my past and that's okay, because my past doesn't determine my future."

> *Our past doesn't determine our future!*

GET TO KNOW YOURSELF

In her book *Bits and Pieces of My Soul,* Dr. Carolyn Dixon wrote, "All things in life begin with you. Therefore, it's important to know who you are, what you are, and that for which you stand!"

Getting to know yourself means making a thorough self-analysis that begins by finding answers to questions such as:

- Who am I?

- What is my purpose?

- What do I value?

- What do I want?

- What are my strengths and weaknesses?

Who Am I?

When answering the "Who am I?" question, do not use labels designed to describe your activities, relationships, age, or physical characteristics, but words describing the inner you; the "you" who is separate and apart from what you do.

Sometimes people, especially women, have a tendency to use words such as, "*mother, wife, middle-aged, overweight, secretary, Christian,* or *daughter*" to describe themselves.

These words are labels. They don't describe the inner you. Examples of words describing the inner you might include *friendly, attentive, positive, assertive, confident, responsible, disciplined, focused, creative, loving,* or *considerate.*

To help you find words to describe the inner you, take a few minutes to complete the questions on the next page.

Exercise: WHO AM I?

In the space below or on a separate sheet of paper, record your responses.

1. When meeting new people, I am: _____

_____

_____

_____

2. Things I love to do for fun are: _____

_____

_____

_____

3. Things I am really good at are: _____

_____

_____

_____

4. My biggest fear is: _____

_____

_____

_____

5. What upsets me most is: _____

_____

_____

_____

6. When I am nervous or scared, I: _____

_____

_____

_____

7. I feel most frustrated when _____

_____

_____

_____

8. I am most productive when: _____

_____

_____

_____

9. My friends/co-workers describe me as:_____

_____

_____

_____

10. Five non-labeling words that describe me are: _____

_____

_____

_____

What Is My Purpose?

Nietzsche once said, "He who knows the why of his life can bear with almost any how." I can safely say that many people don't have a clearly defined purpose. A question I am frequently asked is "How do you find your purpose?"

Though I have no simple or easy answer to this question, at the end of this section, I have included some actions and thought-provoking questions that might help you to define your purpose or life mission.

I stumbled onto my purpose while going through that "I don't know what I want to be when I grow up" stage.

I was thirty-eight years old with a Master's degree in Business Administration. I had held several financially and psychologically unsatisfying jobs. Tired of just taking a job because I needed a job (you may know the feeling), I decided to enroll in a six-week career and life-planning course with a community-based volunteer organization. While participating in the program I became a volunteer myself. Volunteers were required to conduct career-planning workshops. Although I had an intense fear of public speaking (based on the experience mentioned earlier), I somehow found the courage and the confidence to conduct a seminar.

By the end of my first seminar, I knew that I had found my niche, and, shortly thereafter, my purpose, my life mission: *To empower people to improve the quality of their lives.*

Once my purpose was clear, my career and my life just seemed to fall into place. I was no longer searching. I no longer scanned the classified ads looking for the ideal job. I could make my own ideal job. Finally I knew what I wanted to be "when I grew up" – a trainer and a speaker.

I could then focus my attention on developing my skills as a trainer and speaker. I discovered that I had a natural talent for teaching, speaking, and designing workshops and seminars.

Finding my niche at thirty-eight made me one of the lucky ones. Most people go through their entire life not knowing their ultimate calling. Some people never give it much thought, while others agonize over it. I think that I found my niche out of sheer frustration.

Viktor Frankl, author of *Man's Search for Meaning*, stated, "You find the meaning of life [your purpose] by: (1) doing a deed; (2) experiencing a value; and (3) suffering."

Sometimes people resist their purpose. I often think about one of my mentors who, in her early sixties, became a minister and founded her own church. She told me she knew from an early age the "why" of her life. But for years she resisted. Finally, she couldn't "run anymore." Eventually, her ultimate purpose consumed her, occupying her thoughts all of the time.

She often told me that once she acknowledged and embraced her purpose, no matter how difficult and challenging her work became as the pastor of a low-income congregation with many pressing spiritual, emotional, and financial needs, she didn't mind. It gave her life meaning.

That's what happens when you come face-to-face with a purpose that drives you. You forget the pain and the dangers. H. I. Khan stated, "However unhappy a person may be, the moment he knows the purpose of his life a switch is turned and the light is on. If he has to strive after that purpose all his life, he does not mind so long as he knows what the purpose is."

Finding your purpose or life mission can be a daunting task. Here are some actions and thought-provoking questions designed to help you focus on your purpose or life mission.

- Start keeping a daily or weekly journal.

- Read books and articles on the subject of finding your mission, purpose, vocation, or calling.

- Talk to others whom you admire about their purpose and how they were able to determine it.

- Begin thinking and writing what you see as your unique talents and interests. Write your thoughts in your journal.

- Listen to your inner voice or your heart. What is it telling you about the "why" of your life?

- Ask yourself the following questions (recording the responses in your journal):

  a. What has meaning for me?

  b. What talents and skills do I have that I love to use, or that I am not using but would like to use?

c.   If money were not an issue, what would I be doing with my life? What would bring me joy?

d.   What do I see as my purpose or mission?

In the space below or on a separate sheet of paper, write a draft mission or purpose statement that best represents you at this time. This statement need not be "cast in stone." As you think about your purpose and learn more about yourself, refine your statement. Your purpose need not seem "grand" or fame-producing. It should, however, fit your unique personality and abilities, as well as reflect your values.

Our purpose impacts our values. Our values and our purpose impact our wants.

Exercise: DRAFT PURPOSE STATEMENT

The following statement best represents me at this time.

_____

_____

_____

_____

_____

_____

_____

_____

_____

What Do I Value?

Knowing yourself means having a clear understanding of your values – what you stand for and what's really important to you. Values are principles that guide our lives. They define who we are as individuals.

They are made up of everything that has happened to you in your life and include influences from: family, religious affiliation, friends, peers, your education, and a variety of other things. Once defined they impact every aspect of our behavior – the choices and decisions we make, how we are inclined to respond to situations that arise in our lives, and our relationship to ourselves and to others. Yet if you asked the average person to list their top five or ten values, many would struggle to come up with even one.

Whether we are consciously aware of them or not, we all have a core set of values (rules by which we live). These values can range from the usual, such as family, friends, loyalty, God, and health, to the more psychological, such as self-reliance, service to humanity, concern for others, freedom, and harmony of purpose.

Values are unique to each of us. And they can change as our lives and circumstances change. For example, the older I get, the more importance I place on relationships, service, and financial independence. In my early twenties, these were not even among my top five.

As we become clear about our values, it's important that we constantly challenge ourselves by asking, "Is my behavior consistent with what I value?" or "Am I living my values?" If the answer is no, then the next question should be, "Is this principle (value) really important to me?" For example, you list helping others as one of your core values. Yet you rarely, if ever, make any attempt to offer your assistance to anyone. In this instance, your behavior wouldn't be consistent with this value. Our behavior – what we do – normally reflects our values.

What do you value? On the next page is a list of things people value.

Exercise: WHAT DO I VALUE?

In the space provided or on a separate sheet of paper, check five values that are most important to you. Feel free to add your own to this list.

_____ Achievement	_____ Material wealth
_____ Adventure	_____ Meaningful work
_____ Contributing to society	_____ Privacy
_____ Family	_____ Religion
_____ Friends	_____ Reputation
_____ Helping others	_____ Service
_____ Integrity	_____ Trust and honesty

Add your own: _____

_____

_____

_____

_____

_____

_____

_____

_____

What Do I Want?

A want is a desire that is clear and specific.

From now on, you must focus on what you want instead of what others want for you. When you let others define your wants, you are giving them power over your dreams, hopes, and aspirations.

Many people don't know what they want. They only know what they don't want. Before I discovered my life's purpose, I fit into this category. Although I had a Masters degree in Business Administration and a decent job, I had no idea what I wanted to be "when I grew up." When asked what I wanted to do, I could only talk about what I didn't want to do. I remember thinking: *I can do anything if only I knew what it was.*

I once heard Les Brown, a noted motivational speaker, say, "In order to G-E-T, you have to A-S-K." It dawned on me that some of us can't A-S-K because we don't have a clue what we really want. Or our wants are fuzzy and not specific. When we're not clear on what we want, we can't A-S-K. Therefore, we don't G-E-T.

I once asked a friend what she wanted out of life. She responded, "I don't want much. I just want to 'make do.'" I thought to myself, *What a scary thought – going through life "making do."*

The clearer you are about your wants, the easier it is to make them a reality.

If you really don't know what you want, then begin by describing the "lifestyle" you would like to live. Although I had no idea of what I wanted to be "when I grew up," I was quite clear on the lifestyle. I wanted an abundance of every good thing life had to offer – happiness, health, peace of mind, wealth. I knew that I didn't want to live "from paycheck to paycheck," nor did I want to "just get by" financially.

During the period I was discovering my purpose, I wrote out a more detailed description of what I wanted my life to look like. As your purpose grows clearer, so will your list of wants.

What do you want? In the space provided below or on a separate sheet of paper, write down some of the things you really want.

Exercise: WHAT DO I WANT?

List some of your deepest desires. Make them clear and specific.

_____

_____

_____

_____

_____

_____

_____

What Are My Strengths and Weaknesses?

I look at strengths as those things that will move me closer to my ultimate goal. I focus on my strengths. I work to make them stronger by reading, studying, practicing, talking to others, or doing whatever it is I need to do.

I look at weaknesses as those things that may or may not interfere with my ability to get what I want to out of life. If a weakness truly interferes with my ability to get the results I want, I take action to correct it. If it doesn't interfere, I let it go. It's important not to dwell on all the areas we may consider weaknesses, but just those we need to strengthen to achieve our goals.

We could all spend a lifetime trying to alleviate all of our weaknesses, but then a lifetime would be lost. Work only on those things that are central to achieving your goals or that hinder you from getting, doing, or being what you want to be.

A few years ago, a member of my office team decided that I could be more productive if I were more organized. She kept trying to get me organized, setting up all kinds of fancy reporting systems and forms for me to fill out and follow. Finally I insisted that she stop trying to get me organized.

Although being organized is important, it would not make me a better speaker. My time was much better spent improving my skills in training, speaking, listening, writing, and marketing – not trying to be organized. This weakness would not interfere with my ability to achieve my goals as long as I surrounded myself with people who had this skill.

Redefine yourself by identifying your strengths and weaknesses. Then focus on ways to build your strengths.

What are your strengths and weaknesses?

In the space provided or on a separate sheet of paper, identify your strengths and weaknesses. Focus only on those weaknesses that will interfere with your ability to achieve the success you desire.

Exercise: STRENGTHS AND WEAKNESSES

To find your strengths, revisit your *Who Am I* responses.

Strengths: _____

_____

_____

_____

_____

_____

Weaknesses: _____

_____

_____

_____

_____

_____

_____

REWRITE YOUR SCRIPT

After you have made a thorough self-analysis, you are now ready to adjust your picture – to redefine yourself for yourself. You now have the tools to rewrite your script. A script is a series of positive statements that supports and reinforces the qualities you are seeking, or reinforces who you really are.

You begin by making a list of qualities and characteristics you must have in order for you to feel confident directing the course of your life. You will use this list to create a new script for yourself to replace the old one that gets in your way.

Your list might include traits such as calm, self-assured, confident, funny, enthusiastic, passionate, intelligent, positive, cheerful, healthy, happy, successful, or wealthy. You may already have the qualities you desire but want to make them stronger. List those too.

Next, develop a script to affirm these qualities and plant them firmly in your subconscious mind. For example, to reinforce and internalize the qualities of a person who is calm, confident, and self-assured, you are to tell yourself: "I am calm, confident, and self-assured." Not "I am going to be calm, confident, and self-assured," but "I am…"

Write your script and speak to yourself in the present tense, as if you already have the desired qualities.

MY PERSONAL SELF-IMAGE SCRIPT

Here is the script I used to redefine myself and to build a healthier self-image. My script included qualities I desired as well as those I had and wanted to strengthen or reinforce.

"I am calm, confident, and self-assured."

"I am a unique, confident, and interesting person."

"I love who I am, and I feel good about myself."

"I radiate energy, enthusiasm, and love. If you look closely you can even see a glow around me."

"I am a very special person. As a matter of fact, I am extra special."

"The more I love myself, the more I love others."

"I wanted to be somebody, and now I know I am."

"I have many beautiful qualities about me, and I am discovering new ones every day."

"I am intelligent. I am quick, clever, and fun."

"I am happy on the inside and on the outside."

"I am unstoppable."

"I hold positive, prosperity thoughts at all times."

"Good things are always happening to and for me."

"I only maintain relationships that are in my best interest."

Even if these statements apply to you, your script will be more effective when you create your own.

ACT AS IF

After you have a developed a full description of the person you want to be and a script to remind you of your essential qualities, you must *act* and *speak* as if you already have the qualities you desire. To help you "act as if," constantly – in your mind – play your new tape.

Why? If we tell ourselves something long enough, our minds will begin to believe it, whether what we're telling ourselves is something good or something bad. And it's just as easy to tell ourselves positive things as it is to tell ourselves negative things. The problem is we don't believe that, so we continue to tell ourselves negative things.

This is why it's so important to be conscious of our thoughts, feelings, and actions, and not just travel through life on autopilot. In fact, from now on you can treat your mind like a garden. Every time one of your old, negative tapes begins to play, weed it out by "planting" a new, positive script instead. Soon these new messages will take firm hold and begin to bear fruit.

Affirm yourself frequently. A good practice is to tape your script to your mirror and every time you look in the mirror, repeat your script – and mean it. Make it a point to look in the mirror more, even making a special effort to get in front of a mirror as often as possible to re-affirm yourself. Look yourself in the eyes –your big, beautiful eyes – and allow yourself to appreciate your qualities, your potential, and your ability to achieve optimum success.

> *Act the way you want to be,*
> *soon you will be the way you act!*

PICTURE THE NEW YOU

Spend fifteen to thirty minutes a day speaking your script aloud … picturing or visualizing yourself possessing the qualities you would like to have … being the person you would like to be. If you don't have fifteen to thirty minutes, start with five minutes.

Be specific. When you see yourself as the person you want to be, picture what you're doing, who you're with, and how you feel.

Do this affirmation/visualization ritual daily. If you miss a day, don't beat yourself up; simply start over. Without doing anything else, consistent affirming and picturing can dramatically change your whole outlook. Your eyes grow bigger, and the world opens wider too.

MAKE A MOVE

DO SOMETHING! Although consistent affirming and picturing can dramatically change your whole outlook, you still must *do something.* You must put some action behind your words and your pictures. For example:

- If the desired quality is to be outgoing, you must deliberately place yourself in a position to meet and interact with people. This might mean getting out of your comfort zone, going out alone, or striking up a conversation with a perfect stranger.

- If the desired quality is to be calm, you must deliberately take a deep breath and recite an affirmation when you feel your anxiety or temper rising. You may need to exercise more, take a yoga class, or sing with the radio instead of yelling at an aggressive driver.

- If the desired quality is to be self-assured, you must deliberately speak up, stick to your values, and let others know where you stand. This may mean taking a risk with your boss, a friend, or a loved one. You may need to practice in front of that mirror!

You don't have to dive in head first. Take small steps for starters, and work your way up to bigger steps.

Make a conscious effort every day to take actions that will move you closer to your goals and enable you to redefine yourself as the person you aspire to be.

THE POWER OF AFFIRMATIONS

To reinforce the power of positive affirmations, following is an excerpt from a letter I received from a workshop participant.

Dear Daisy,

I just wanted to thank you and let you know how helpful your personal self-image script is. At the time I attended your class, my daughter was having a severe "self-esteem" problem. She was in the pits. I gave her your script and shared your comments about retraining the mind – that the mind believes anything you tell it if you say it enough times. She really didn't believe me. Some time later I found the script taped to her mirror. I no longer hear her moaning and groaning negative self-put-downs. Last evening she was talking on the telephone to a friend. She was spouting the same advice I had given her. "Use self-talk. The mind believes whatever you tell it." I just wanted you to know that your information doesn't fall on deaf ears and it goes much further than the classroom.

Again, thanks.

Key Points to Remember

You can unlearn a negative self-image. It doesn't matter when the negative messages started, where they came from, or how deeply entrenched they are. With practice and diligence you can erase or unlearn those old, self-defeating messages.

☻

Be aware of past programming. Understand the events and experiences (good or bad) that shaped or influenced your life. Make them work *for,* not against, you.

☻

Your past does not determine your future.

☻

Everybody has an opinion, usually about everything, and especially about what *you* should or should not, cannot, or will not do. No one knows you better than you know yourself. Don't let anyone tell you who you are and what's best for you – make that determination for yourself. You and only you should define who you are.

☻

It is up to you to create a new script for your life. Make a list of qualities you must have in order for you to feel confident directing the course of your life.

☻

Act the way you want to be; soon you will be the way you act.

❧

On a daily basis, picture yourself having the qualities you desire. Picture your new and powerful self-image.

❧

Take actions that reinforce the positive messages that you feed yourself. *Do something!*

Believe...that you are all of the things you aspire to be.

Think on This: What qualities would you like to develop or enhance? How would you feel having these desired qualities? What would you be doing? Who would you be with?

Act on This: Develop a self-talk script to reinforce the person you just imagined. Then look yourself in your big eyes and say your script out loud several times a day and whenever you need a reminder. Going into a meeting? Say your script. Meeting someone new? *Act as if.*

Chapter 3:

HAVE A CLEAR VISION

See the Possibilities with Big Eyes

Where there is no vision, the people perish.

- Proverbs 29:18

Vision is the capacity to believe in what the heart sees, what others can't see. Vision is seeing positive possibilities where others see only negative possibilities.

- Carl A. Hammerschlag

SEEING THE POSSIBILITIES

Now that you've examined the picture you have of yourself and dealt with the negative messages that hinder you from achieving optimum success, it's time to widen your eyes to take in the bigger picture. It's time to start looking at your life, and the vision you have for your life.

Vision is simply seeing beyond the present moment, seeing the big picture, seeing into the future – seeing the possibilities.

As a child, I was blessed with vision. We didn't have television, but we had books and store catalogs. I was always an avid reader. I always had big dreams for myself. And while I had never seen much of it, I knew there was a world outside of Quincy, Florida. I knew there was a world beyond the tobacco fields and outhouses and dirt roads – a world I wanted to taste and touch and experience; a world I wanted to see with my own big eyes.

While other children used their free time, what little there was, to run and play and jump, you could always find me curled up in a corner somewhere with my nose in a book.

One of my favorite things to do was to flip through the pages of the Sears catalog and point out all of the beautiful things I would have some day – shiny new shoes and pretty dresses that were store bought and no one else had worn.

One day, lost and daydreaming in my catalog world, I overheard two elderly women visiting my parents say, "Something is wrong with her. Her eyes are too big." Although I did and do have big eyes, I realized that the women were not really talking about the size of my eyes. They were talking about the size of my dreams. They were the vocal minority of a silent majority who considered me "touched in the head," a term meaning mentally slow or not quite right.

Those women, like many of the people in that small town, couldn't, or wouldn't, allow themselves to dream. Many were born, raised, married, had their babies, and died in Quincy, without having ever seen much of the world beyond rural Florida.

I was a dreamer. And that made me a pariah, an outcast. But there's good to be found in every seemingly bad situation. Sometimes it's not until many years later, when we connect the dots of our lives, that we discover the good in what seemed at the time to be adversity.

Even as a child I had the ability to recognize and take advantage of a blessing when one came my way. Because I was labeled slow, I was given a job in the tobacco processing operation that didn't require any great mental ability. And that left me plenty of time to dream, and plan, and plot, if you will, the life I knew I would some day lead outside of Quincy. While I didn't define it as such back then, I was developing my vision.

OTHERS CAN'T ALWAYS SEE YOUR VISION!

Some years later, although I carried a very high grade point average in high school, my parents were strongly advised by the overseer of the tobacco farm not to send me to college. That man couldn't see my vision, and likely had his own selfish reasons for discouraging my parents from sending me to college. He probably never even considered that a poor, skinny little black girl could or would even dare to dream, to have vision.

Those elderly women also didn't understand or consider that I might have had vision; their eyes were too small. All the overseer and those women could see was what was in front of them, literally. They certainly couldn't be expected to see, understand, or support my vision.

Don't let others' inability to see or understand your vision keep you from having and achieving your dreams. When your children, spouse, or friends confide their dreams to you, never scoff or naysay. Encourage their dreams and tell them they can achieve all they set their minds and hearts to. Then tell yourself the same thing – often.

VISION IS A WALK OF FAITH

Having vision means having faith. It means being able to see and recognize the possibilities. We all start life as visionaries – big-eyed creatures with the ability to dream and travel in our minds to heights we've never known *except* in our minds. How else do you explain imaginary playmates – those friends no one else can see, but to whom we give names and invite to tea parties, or whose space on the sofa we protect? As children, when we're allowed to dream, to fantasize and have vision, we are given a license to succeed, to go after all that God has waiting for us.

But too often, as we get older, we allow the naysayers to smother our dreams, extinguishing the passion. Because we are told that we cannot, should not, will not, and could not, we pack our dreams away. We choose the mediocre, but safe path.

Having vision also means having a sense of daring. Daring doesn't necessarily mean doing crazy things. I could have conformed after overhearing the elderly women say that my eyes were too big. I could have put away the catalogs and joined the other children – chosen the safe route. I dared to be different.

Lack of vision – narrow eyes – is one of the greatest barriers to getting what we deserve and what we as human beings were intended to have. We become so immersed in our current drama that we fail to take the time to see and plan for the future. Lack of vision causes people to stay in abusive relationships, in jobs they hate, in poverty and despair. Some people have what I refer to as a limited vision. They place restrictions on themselves. They "see" small, using as an excuse the desire to be realistic.

In workshops, I often remind people that it's okay to dream big, to want material things. Often it seems that people are surprised to hear this, as if it were a sin to want big things – big houses, nice cars, fulfilling relationships, and all the other goodies that we as human beings are entitled to.

To achieve optimum success it's important to have a clear vision of what *you* want your future and your legacy to look like. While I was blessed to be born with vision, it's something anyone can develop.

How? Begin by thinking like a child. Don't censor your dreams. What is it that you want, what are your desires? What do you aspire to be, do, or have? Open your eyes as wide as you can – the sky is the limit. See the possibilities. If you need help imagining the possibilities, read books and magazines, go to movies, take courses, expand your circle of friends, daydream, meditate, talk to someone you trust, travel to and explore new places, or volunteer.

CREATE A PVS – PERSONAL VISION STATEMENT

When you're able to see the possibilities, it's then time to create a Personal Vision Statement. The statement doesn't have to be long or complicated; in fact, simple and to-the-point is even better. Your PVS can reflect your core values, what you want your future to look like, or what you personally aspire to be, have, or do. It generally answers the question, "What are you all about?" in a very broad way. Your vision statement is yours and it's personal. Only *you* can define what it is.

For instance, my Personal Vision Statement is to positively influence others to grow and prosper in all areas of their lives. Other examples of PVS are:

"To make others laugh."

"To promote healthy relationships."

"To actively promote equity and harmony between people from diverse backgrounds."

"To heal."

One of the most compelling vision statements of the 20th century can be found in Dr. Martin Luther King, Jr.'s, August 1963, *I Have a Dream* speech. His vision was "an America free of bias, intolerance, and injustice."

To help you formulate your PVS, some key questions to consider are:

- What motivates you or brings you joy?

- Why are you here? What is your life purpose?

- What are your core values?

- What do you want to be, do, or have?

- What would you do if money were not a factor?

- What are you most passionate about?

As you begin to answer these questions, key words will start to emerge. Use those words to help you develop and focus your Personal Vision Statement.

A compelling vision helps to keep you focused and on track. It drives you and inspires those around you.

Key Points to Remember

Expand your vision. See beyond the present moment.

❂

Vision is a skill that anyone can learn, or relearn.

❂

Don't let others' inability to see or understand your vision keep you from having and achieving it.

❂

Open your eyes as wide as you can – the sky is the limit.

❂

Start formulating your vision by allowing yourself to daydream again. Make and take time each day to let yourself dream.

❂

A compelling vision keeps you focused, on track, and inspires you as well as those around you.

❂

Dream Big!

Believe…that whatever you envision,
you can have, be, or do.

Think on This: What does your vision world look like? What do you do in your vision world? What is your PVS?

Act on This: Envision your ideal future with your eyes open wide. Go ahead, write it, sketch it, or collage it from magazines or books. Let your creativity have a field day. Don't judge or censor yourself. You're allowed to want what you want. **DREAM BIG!**

Chapter 4:
SET GOALS
Keep Your Big Eyes Clear

A goal is a dream with a deadline.

- Napoleon Hill

Nothing is as real as a dream.
The world can change around you, but your dream will not.
Responsibilities need not erase it. Duties need not obscure it.
Because the dream is within you, no one can take it away.

- Unknown

Once you have a clear vision of what optimum success looks like to you, it's time to narrow that vision by asking yourself, "What do I *really* want?" When you can answer that question, it's then time to set goals – to develop a plan. It's almost impossible to talk about achieving success without discussing the importance of planning and setting goals.

How many times have you heard, "Failing to plan is planning to fail"? Yes, this is an old, established cliché but nonetheless true.

Many people don't create a plan, a road map, for their lives. They believe that "fate" is in control, that whatever is going to be is going to be and there's nothing they can do about it. But the reality is that those who rise to the top – who achieve lasting success – do so because they have a plan for their lives. And that plan involves setting and achieving specific goals.

Think of your goals as a target. To hit the target you 1) Take aim – create a plan; 2) Shoot – implement your plan; 3) Score – achieve the goal.

Most people spend more time planning a party, a vacation, or a wedding than they do planning their lives.

If you don't plan, life just happens. And sometimes that's a good thing, just letting life happen. Like spending a Saturday just letting the day take you where it will, or nowhere at all. But that's not a way to live your entire life. In fact, that's a reckless way to live your life.

People who fail to plan end up living from paycheck to paycheck. They end up in jobs, rather than careers. They wake up one day realizing they've grown old and never accomplished the things they dreamed about, but never planned for.

In my goal-setting workshops, I ask for a show of hands of people who are working at jobs or who are in careers that they deliberately set out to be in – that they planned and worked toward. More often than not, very few hands go up.

Many of us –too many, in fact – are working jobs or in the midst of careers that we stumbled into. Many people are stuck in situations they landed in because they needed to pay the bills and the organization they work for was hiring. Often I hear people say, "I only meant to stay a year." Twenty years later, they're still there. Surveys show that many people are in jobs they don't even like.

Most of us spend more time working than doing anything else. We spend so much time working, and so much of our life revolves around work, that not liking what we do for a living equates to spending the majority of our life doing something we don't want to be doing, at a place we probably don't like going. In short, we spend major portions of our lives in a state of frustration, anxiety, or unhappiness. You don't have to have an M.D. behind your name to figure that that's not good.

Does the situation described above describe your life? It was how I described my life at one time. Prior to starting my own training and consulting firm, I fit squarely in this category.

In my teens, motivated by my desire to not spend the rest of my life working in the tobacco fields, my goal was to go to college. But that was goal-setting created out of desperation, and unfortunately that was where my goal-setting began and ended. Like many young people, I assumed that once I had a degree in hand everything else would fall into place. Things fell into place all right – but not a place my big eyes would ever have imagined or chosen. So at age thirty-eight I found myself in a job that wasn't satisfying – psychologically or financially.

Through a series of life-altering events – which included discovering my life purpose – I figured out what I wanted to do with my life and what success looked like to me. It was then that I started to fully understand the benefits of goal-setting. And I began setting goals for myself. I often wonder now how different my life might be today if I had been goal-oriented in my early twenties. But it's never too late to change, and the rewards of goal-setting are certainly worth it, whenever you start.

Some of the benefits of setting goals include:

- **Peace of mind.** There is a certain satisfaction to taking control of your destiny. Goal-setting increases your chances of getting what you want.

- **Focus.** Having and working toward a set of goals helps keep you focused on the important things.

- **Sense of direction.** Goal-setting helps you to know where you are going and what you need to do to get there.

- **Sense of personal fulfillment.** Setting and achieving goals is a measure of personal success, and personal success is one of the best self-esteem boosters we can give ourselves.

- **Career satisfaction.** You'll be in the driver's seat, able to *choose* positions that give you more personal satisfaction, and likely pay more.

- **Ongoing motivation.** Setting goals is an instant motivator. It forces you to be responsible for your own life – for both successes and failures.

Although the benefits of setting goals are enormous and the consequences of not setting goals are dire, many people – too many, in fact – don't set goals. I believe that often people don't set goals because they don't know how, were never taught how, and don't realize the value of goal-setting.

As a child growing up in the deep south, no one ever talked to me or each other about goals. Of course they had goals, things like keeping food on the table and a roof over our heads, but that was called survival! The importance of goal-setting wasn't mentioned in my high school, nor do I remember anyone mentioning it while I was in college. I learned the true meaning and benefits of goal-setting much later. But again, it's never too late to transform or improve your life.

Now that you know the importance of goal-setting, there's no excuse for putting off doing it. Here are seven guidelines for helping you set goals:

☞ **Put your goals in writing.** Goal-setting begins with knowing what you want. A goal in writing represents commitment. It forces you to stop and really think about who you are, what you want, and how you would like to live your life. Putting your goals in writing adds clarity; it gives you something to refer back to, and something to measure. It also enables you to review your goals regularly, and it gives them energy. A goal that's not in writing is merely a wish. How much energy do you put behind a wish? We don't approach a wish with the same intensity, energy, enthusiasm, and commitment as we do a goal that's in writing.

➲ **Make sure your goals are clear and specific.** When the goal is clear and specific, you have an idea of what you must do to make it happen. A specific goal serves as your road map. The more specific the goal, the less time you will waste on activities that are unrelated to what you're trying to accomplish. "To be successful," "To be happy," or "To be financially secure" are starting points, but not nearly specific enough. They don't describe exactly what you desire. An example of a clear and specific goal is "To save at least $5,000 by the end of the year." The clearer the goal, the easier it is to develop a workable action plan and to picture or visualize success. Fuzzy, unclear goals lead to fuzzy actions and outcomes, as well as wasted time.

➲ **Have a target date.** Goals should be anchored to a timetable. A target date serves two main purposes: First, it's one way to stay on track and second it allows you to measure at any given time whether you are on track. You will work harder and more consistently on a goal with a target date. Without a target date, it's easy to procrastinate or get distracted by the responsibilities of daily living. Some of us give up when we don't reach our goal by the specified target date. If you don't reach your goal by the target date, don't give up. Review your goal. If it's something you really desire, take the necessary corrective actions, if any, and simply set another target date.

➲ **Make sure your goal is measurable in objective terms.** If the goal isn't measurable, you will not know what you are aiming for, nor will you know when you've reached your goal. For example, how can a goal "to be happy" be measured? It can't, because there are no standards by which you can measure progress. Look back at the goal "to save at least $5,000 by the end of the year." Not only is this goal clear and specific, with a target date, it can be objectively measured.

👁 **Make your goal realistic and attainable.** Goals must be realistic and attainable based on your mental and physical capacity to achieve them. And they must be compatible with where you are in your life. Otherwise, you are committing self-sabotage by setting yourself up for failure. For example, if you're living from paycheck to paycheck, barely making ends meet, it's probably not realistic to set a goal of saving $5,000 by year-end.

In terms of your goal being attainable, I believe that if you have the mental and physical capacity, anything is possible. If you can think it and truly believe it, you can do it.

A story I read in the *Baltimore Sun* newspaper clearly reinforces this belief. According to the story, a former high school cheerleader made a list of ten things she wanted to accomplish before she died. The list included becoming an NFL cheerleader. In the spring of 2005, she auditioned for the Baltimore Ravens – and made the squad. What's so unique about this? This former cheerleader was a thirty-eight-year-old married woman with three children under the age of seven. At the time she auditioned and made the cheerleading squad, the average age for Ravens cheerleaders was twenty-three. She became the oldest professional cheerleader in the team's history. Undoubtedly, this young woman knew that in spite of her age and family responsibilities, she had the desire as well as the mental and physical ability to accomplish her goal. And she believed. William James, the great American philosopher said it best: "Our belief at the beginning of a doubtful undertaking is the one thing that assures the successful outcome."

👁 **Make sure your goals are *your* goals.** Goals are personal. They must be within your ability to control. They must focus on what you want, not what others want for you. Our parents, our friends, our spouses, co-workers, and others often offer advice on what they think we need or will make us happy. Often this advice is unsolicited and given without hesitation.

No matter how well someone else knows you, or how long they've known you, they are on the outside looking in. It's up to you to decide what's best for you. Do take the opinions of others – those who know you best – into consideration. Do investigate the possibilities. Do think out-of-the-box and beyond what you can or have seen, even if the people around you can't or haven't seen it or don't understand. Do become the master of your fate and take ownership of your life by setting goals that are yours - and *yours alone.*

👁 **Make sure you can picture the end results.** If you can conceive it, believe it, and see it, you can be, do, or have it. Visualization works! Visualization is using your mind's eye to create the picture of what you want in your life. This is a goal achieving technique that has been around for centuries. Les Brown, renowned motivational speaker and author, stated, "You must see your goals clearly and specifically before you can set out for them. Hold them in your mind until they become second nature."

For years people from all walks of life have been using visualization to reach their goals. We have all heard stories of athletes using the technique of visualizing before an event. The athletes see themselves winning in their minds' eye. They win the event before it even begins. We have also read stories of athletes and businesspeople using visualization to improve their performance.

Whether we realize it or not, we visualize without even thinking about it. I often refer to it as daydreaming. As children, when we dressed up and played nurse or doctor or schoolteacher, we were visualizing our future in a physical way.

Visualization is not only a powerful technique for reaching goals, it is also used to build self-confidence and self-esteem, to learn or master a new skill, to manage stress, to handle conflict, to deal with a variety of issues and challenges, including health-related challenges, and to improve performance.

I used visualization daily to help me to overcome my fear of public speaking.

I would take a few minutes each day, get in a relaxed state, and picture myself speaking confidently to a large audience. I would visualize this when I woke up in the morning and just before I went to sleep at night. In my mind's eye, I would see the audience, their smiles and laughter, see myself walking around on the platform, hear the applause, and feel the warmth emanating from the audience. It was as if I were watching a movie with me being on center stage. Sometimes before visualizing my goal, I would write out a detailed scenario of what

I would be doing when I realized my goal. I would write as if I had already achieved the goal. Writing out the scenario gave me a clearer picture.

ACHIEVING YOUR GOALS

Achieving your goals begins with your thoughts – developing a consciousness to know that you can reach your desired goal. You must deliberately spend time just thinking about your goal. You must have an intense or burning desire. Your desire could be equated to an obsession.

Contrary to what some may think, obsession is not a dirty word; it simply means that you are passionate about what you want. You must truly believe that your goal is achievable. No matter the odds, you must believe.

You may encounter some roadblocks or barriers when attempting to reach your goals. These roadblocks may include lack of self-confidence, not having the right skills or necessary education, limited finances, time, health issues, family commitments, lack of support, fear, and indecision. But most of these barriers can be overcome. They will only stop you if you let them!

Only you can stop you from reaching your goals.

Oftentimes, we don't reach our goals because we never believed they were possible. We doubt ourselves. When we doubt ourselves, we sabotage ourselves. Other reasons we sometimes don't reach our goals may include:

◉ **We don't surround ourselves with the right support system.** It's important that we surround ourselves with people who encourage, support, and when necessary, challenge us – always in the direction of our goals. *Beware of the naysayers or dream stealers* – people who try to discourage you or steal your dreams.

◉ **We give up too quickly.** It takes courage to keep working toward your goals. When you feel that you want to give up on your goals – and many people do – persist. You may be closer than you think. Sometimes even I get tired and frustrated and want to give up. When this happens, I take time out to read a poem or an inspirational book, or listen to a motivational audio learning program for encouragement.

Here is one of my favorite meditations that encourages me to keep on striving.

Don't Give Up!
Your Dreams May Be Closer Than You Think!

There may be times when you feel
as if you have taken a million steps towards
your dreams, and acted on your plans, only to find
yourself in the same place that you began from.
At times like this, you must not give up.

You must continue on. Though you may feel
lost, bewildered, and alone, continue to believe
in yourself. Do not allow discouragement and
doubt to blur your vision and wash away
your dreams. Visualize your way beyond the
detours, standstills, and obstacles.

You will realize your dreams. You have
worked hard and taken so many productive
steps in a positive direction that you are bound
to succeed. Whatever the hurt of the moment
may be, it will pass. Tomorrow is always a
new dawn. Today, you must pause, rest, catch
your breath, and then look ahead. Each step
will bring you closer to your dreams. The
rainbows and the love that you deserve are in
sight. Happiness is just around the next turn.

-Vicki Silvers, Poet

SOME FINAL THOUGHTS ON GOALS

Goals are classified as short-term, intermediate, long-term, and lifetime goals. Our goals should cover every area of our lives – personal, career, health, financial, and spiritual. And they should be aligned with your values and your vision.

Make goal-setting a family affair. Goal-setting is a life-long skill that will give your children a head start in the game of life. Whether your children are in elementary, middle, or high school, setting goals can help motivate and keep them on track. Teach them early how to set and attain goals.

Key Points to Remember

Make a commitment to yourself and your goals by putting them in writing.

❦

Clear and specific goals are easier to picture and to achieve.

❦

Fuzzy goals lead to fuzzy actions, outcomes, and pictures.

❦

If you can dream it, you can be, do, or have it, if you are willing to put forth the effort.

❦

Don't give up on your dreams – you may be closer than you think.

❦

It takes courage to keep working toward your goals.

❦

Make goal-setting a family affair.

❦

Visualize success. Take time each day to visualize yourself as the successful person you will be once you have achieved your goals.

Believe...that success starts with a belief! As with anything you set out to achieve in this life, you must truly believe that despite your current or past circumstances, despite all the odds and the people who tell you differently, you can and will reach your goals!

Think on This: What are your dreams (goals) in the key areas of your life? What's stopping you from achieving your dreams?

Act on This: Make a list of your goals in each area of your life: personal, career, health, financial, and spiritual. Make sure your goals align with your values and your vision. Next, begin to list specific steps you can take to reach those goals – and take those first steps! Begin today.

Chapter 5:

FOCUS

Keep Your Big Eyes on the Prize

Whatever you steadfastly direct your attention to, will come into your life and dominate it. If you do not direct your attention to anything in particular – and many people do not – then nothing in particular will come into your life except uncertainty and suspense.

- Emmet Fox

F-O-C-U-S – five letters that can stand between you and optimum success.

Focus is determination coupled with a goal and single-mindedness about reaching that goal. It's the identification of the prize (goal) – whatever your prize may be – and the ability to keep your big eyes on that prize. But simply keeping your eyes on the prize isn't enough. You also have to figure out the straightest and most efficient path to take to get to the prize (achieve the goal).

Successful people use the "F" word all the time. Think about it. How many times, when asked during interviews to reveal the secret of their success, have you heard successful people say "focus"? Athletes, actors, authors, scholars, and others almost always attribute their success, in whole or part, to staying focused on their goal.

Vital to our ability to stay focused is our ability to eliminate distractions.

A LITTLE SELFISHNESS GOES A LONG WAY

Life is full of distractions, people and things that can cause us to lose focus, and thus our ability to succeed. Friends and family can be well meaning, but not necessarily a positive influence or conducive to our success. In other words, they can become the distraction that stands between us and success.

How often have you set a goal to get something accomplished, maybe spend an evening completing a project, only to have a friend or family member invite you out, or invite themselves over? These people don't know how to take NO! for an answer. *"You need to get out and have some fun,"* they'll say. Or, *"I'll just stop by for a brief visit."*

Two hours later they're still there, the evening is just about gone, and achieving your goal has been pushed back another day or two or three. Sometimes it's not that you're not fully able or smart enough or committed enough to achieve your goals – it may be that you're not selfish or single-minded enough.

A BIT OF SINGLE-MINDEDNESS IS A GOOD THING

Single-minded is not to be confused with simple-minded. Some people view single-minded people as boring or dull because these people have a tendency to devote all of their time and energies to one thing. They make that one thing their top priority to the exclusion of everything else. But that's not always a bad thing, especially when it comes to achieving your goals. Being single-minded can be a vice or a virtue. On the other hand, not being single-minded enough can cost you.

Take my friend Mike, for example. He is the smartest and most talented person I know. He can write, speak, negotiate, and mediate. He is down-to-earth, caring, and humorous. He reeks of energy, enthusiasm, confidence, and success. He is a "go to" person. He's the one we go to if we need to brainstorm any sort of problem, personally or professionally; if we want an idea generating session or want to know how to do something, or just want a good belly laugh.

One day I said to him, "Mike, you are the smartest person I know."

"Daisy, you're not the first person to tell me that," he responded. "But if I'm so smart, then why am I not a multi-millionaire?"

I didn't answer him right away, but I did spend a good deal of time thinking about the question. Some time later the subject came up in another conversation. We decided that there was one major factor standing between Mike and his dreams of great wealth – a lack of focus. Although Mike is probably a genius, he never focused on or stayed with any one thing in particular. He jumped from one opportunity to another. Had he been more focused and single-minded enough to stay with one thing for a given length of time, today he would be in the multi-millionaire category.

My friend Ed, on the other hand, is a member of the seven-digit club – a multi-millionaire. While in high school he worked in a tool and die shop. He soon found that not only was he good at making small tools, he liked it. After high school he went into the military instead of college. While in the service he discovered that he was very good at a number of other things, including leadership. But wisely, he made the decision to *focus* on the one thing he enjoyed the most – making tools.

When he left the military at age twenty-two, Ed started his own manufacturing company, specializing in small tools for aircraft engines and medical instruments. He stayed with this for more than forty years, ultimately becoming recognized as a leader in his field. He found his niche and he stayed focused on the thing he liked and did best.

With so many things happening around you and to you, it's easy to lose focus, especially when you're good at a lot of things. Some people are easily bored. Some think that they need to be all things to all people, never saying "no". I think that many people make the mistake of trying to be a Jack-of-all-trades. And we all know that didn't even work for Jack.

Remember when Jack and Jill went up the hill? "Jack fell down and broke his crown." That's probably because he was trying to do too many things at once and not focusing on getting the water down the hill. He probably picked up his pail of water before he had focused in on his path or was clear on his purpose. As a result he broke his crown, and probably a few bones, too.

Many people think that the more things they can do, the more productive and profitable they will be. Quite the opposite is true.

"Multi-tasking" is one of those concepts we've all bought into because we think it makes us look smarter, faster, better. In truth, multi-tasking results in more stress and maybe a lot of things getting done – but fewer things being done well. How can you do things well when you're only half focused on them?

It's more important, and more prudent, to be the master of one or two things. The word *master* in itself denotes having control or having great and exemplary skill. It takes time to master true skill. While we're all born with one talent or another, in order to be mastered that talent must be nurtured and developed. Don't try to be a Jack-of-all trades. Master one thing at a time. Then, if you choose, move to another.

People who are focused win the race. Here are some strategies for getting and staying focused.

👁 **Know what you want.** Be clear on what you truly want to do, have, or be. Again, not what others want for you but what you want for yourself. *It's your life.*

👁 **Stay with one thing.** Identify a topic, skill, talent, or hobby you'll enjoy doing for some time to come and *focus* your energies on mastering that topic, skill, talent, or hobby. Make sure that it aligns with your values and vision. Immerse yourself in your chosen area. Learn as much as you can. Become an expert. I define an expert as someone who knows more about a given area of interest than most people.

What do Warren Buffett, Martha Stewart, Dan Poynter, Keith Harrell, and my neighbor, Tom Pazder, have in common? They all stayed with one thing and distinguished themselves as experts in their chosen field. Warren Buffet, considered the greatest investor in American history, is an expert in the area of high finance. Martha Stewart is the internationally known Grand Dame of Hospitality. Dan Poynter is the guru of self-publishing; Keith Harrell is a motivational speaker who is known internationally as "Dr. Attitude". And Tom Pazder was the point man for operational policies and procedures for a major brokerage firm.

Some of these people have international name recognition, some don't. You don't have to have international or national recognition to be an expert. Many people who have distinguished themselves as experts are only known within their industry, their local community, in their field, or within their company.

For example my neighbor, Tom, became known for his expertise within his company. Early on, he had a clear vision of what success looked like to him. Beginning in high school, he worked in the operations department of a major brokerage firm, holding a series of entry-level, low-paying jobs in the back office.

Motivated by his vision of himself, which included wearing "nice clothes to work" and being affiliated with a large prestigious brokerage firm, he decided to learn every job in the back office of the operations department as well as the organization's policies and procedures. The firm had two, three-and-a-half-inch thick manuals: one for policies and one for procedures. He studied and memorized, in their entirety, both manuals. Whenever there was a question regarding the policies or procedures, he was the point man. Later, he expanded his expertise to include handling people problems.

Throughout his career, he received numerous opportunities in operations and elsewhere because he knew more about the firm's operation and its policies and procedures than anyone else and he knew how to manage people. He could have worked in other areas, but he stayed with operations – clearly establishing himself in his chosen field, in his company. Today he is living the life he dreamed because he did those things that were necessary to achieve lasting and optimum success.

☞ **Have a compelling goal.** Have goals that make you want to get out of bed early each morning, goals that keep you putting one foot in front of the other even when your dreams seem light-years away. A compelling goal is one that you live and breathe. It's a goal that's in your heart and soul. You think about it, you talk about it and share it with your loved ones, you dream about it, and you see yourself being, doing, or having whatever that goal is.

When you have a compelling goal, you tend to overlook things that would normally get a negative reaction out of you. You can ignore chaos, uncertainties, and distractions. One of my favorite stories that underscores the power of focus came from a workshop participant.

Early in my career as a trainer, I was conducting a workshop for employees at a major university. There was one participant who was upbeat, positive, and never complained about anything, no matter what was going on at the university. One of her co-workers remarked, "She makes me sick. She acts as if she's oblivious to what's going on around here."

At that time people were being laid off, promotions and raises were frozen, and a freeze had been placed on hiring, all due to budget cuts. People felt overworked and underpaid. Yet this young woman remained positive and upbeat, seeming not to mind the extra work.

What kept her motivated and enthusiastic? She shared her story with the class. She told us that when she was thirteen years old, she decided that she would be a lawyer when she grew up. By the time she graduated from high school, she had fallen in love. She got married right away to her high school sweetheart. She started her family. Still, the desire to be lawyer wouldn't go away. She renewed her goal to be a lawyer. She couldn't afford to go to college, so she started looking around for a place to work where she could get a free education. She targeted a local university with a law school. She told us that the personnel office got tired of her calling and stopping by to see if there were any job openings – any kind of job. "Finally," she said, "they hired me as a clerk typist. I had my foot in the door."

When this young woman showed up in my workshop, it was eight years later in April, and she was getting ready to graduate from law school in May. She was a woman with a compelling goal that kept her focused on the end product – a law degree.

When I heard this young woman's story, it reminded me of a comment by Stephen Covey in his book, *The 7 Habits of Highly Effective People*: "Begin with the end in mind."

This young woman began her quest with the end in mind. She kept her big eyes on the prize: a law degree. No matter what was going on in her life, she could see the light at the end of the tunnel. That's the power of a compelling goal coupled with focus.

When you have a compelling purpose and goal, you tend to approach life with passion, enthusiasm, and excitement – the three keys to lasting and optimum success.

 Eliminate distractions. Learn to just say *NO!* People who are supportive of you and your goals will take no for an answer. Turn off the phone, the television, and the radio; forget, at least for awhile, about multi-tasking; and turn all of your attention and energies toward accomplishing your goals. Set aside time when you will do nothing but focus on your goal. Find a special place – the library, the beach, a closet – anyplace where you can *focus* on your compelling goal.

● **Have a support group.** Make sure your support group is made up of people who have similar goals and objectives. To help me to stay focused, I have aligned myself with others who have either published or are in the process of publishing. I also align myself with success-oriented people who have big eyes and big dreams. From these people, I get support, encouragement, inspiration, and new ideas.

● **Regularly question yourself.** Check in with yourself early and often to make sure that you're on task and on target. Regularly questioning yourself keeps you in the present moment. Ask yourself,

● Is this the best use of my time?

● Is what I am doing related to my purpose, my compelling goals?

Key Points to Remember

The lack of focus can stand between you and optimum success.

👁

People who are focused win the race.

👁

To be focused, you must be clear on what you want to do, have, or be.

👁

Stay with one thing and play it for all it is worth. Become an expert.

👁

Don't let distractions get in your way. Say NO!

👁

Have a compelling goal – a goal that you live and breathe.

👁

Regularly question yourself.

Believe ...that if you focus on your dreams, plan your work, and work your plan, you can achieve your dreams!

Think on This: What interferes with your ability to stay focused on your major goals? In what area (topic, skill, talent, or hobby) can you establish yourself as an expert?

Act on This: List your most common distractions. Now come up with strategies to eliminate or minimize these distractions. Next, list what you will need to do to establish yourself as an expert in your chosen area (topic, skill, talent, or hobby). Do you need to take more courses? Write a book or publish a newsletter? Teach and speak more? Practice more?

C h a p t e r   6 :

BUILD RELATIONSHIPS

Surround Yourself
with Big-Eyed People

Some people enter our lives and leave almost instantly.
Others stay, and forge such an impression on our
heart and soul, we are changed forever.

- Unknown

A reason, a season, a lifetime...

People come in three basic denominations – a season, a reason, or a lifetime. Our challenge is to determine who fits where, and for how long. Surrounding ourselves with the right people can help ensure a good life, filled with success and great experiences. Birds of a feather flock together. If we surround ourselves with big-eyed people – people who believe in our vision, who are positive, who have goals and aspirations and believe in themselves – it stands to reason we, too, will develop those positive qualities.

Conversely, surrounding ourselves with the wrong people can be detrimental to our health, wealth, and well-being, and impede our success. And if we surround ourselves with people who are going nowhere fast...

Some people come into our lives for a short time – a season during which we grow or change. These people bring something to our lives that helps us navigate this transitional period. But when the season has passed, they typically move out of our lives or fade from view.

Sometimes people come into our lives for a reason. They come to teach us something, to guide us, to help us determine what we want, or don't want. Sometimes the reason they were in our lives isn't clear to us until long after they've left our lives. Sometimes the reasons are never fully understood.

Sometimes people are a part of our lives for our entire life. This group may include parents and siblings, long-term friends, and our spouses. They are the lifetimers.

> *People come into our lives for a reason, a season, or a lifetime.*

On the list of things we need to help us reach our potential is to make sure that we surround ourselves with the right people. The people we "hang with" are as important to our ability to reach our goals as are being in the right frame of mind, having vision and focus, and setting realistic and obtainable goals.

Relationships must be nurtured, but just as importantly they must be nurturing. We sometimes do ourselves harm by involving ourselves in relationships that aren't in our best interests. We try to hang on to people whose season in our lives has passed or who've fulfilled the reason or purpose for which they were brought into our lives. When the season is over, whether it lasted for a week or two or many years, it's time to let go. Often we know that the season is over, but we don't want to let go. Even when the relationship has gone toxic, we sometimes try to hang on.

It's important to cultivate our relationships, but it's just as important to know when to move on. And though this is something we don't want to think or believe, sometimes we allow the people who, because of birth or some other reason, will always be a part of our lives have too much influence on our lives. Because someone is "blood" doesn't necessarily mean they have your best interests at heart or should be part of your inner circle – your so-called sphere of influence.

We should always be open to new people coming into our lives. Conversely, we should always be willing and able to close the door on relationships that are toxic. Take a moment and think about the quality of your closest relationships. Do the people in your inner circle love, nourish, and nurture you? Do they challenge you when you need to be challenged, make you want to better yourself, grow, and reach beyond what you thought possible? Do they support your dreams and aspirations? Do they respect the boundaries you set, hear and respect you when you say "no"?

Or do they drain you? When you leave them, do you feel diminished, deflated or unworthy? Do they tell you "You can't" or "You're not ____ enough" or "You're dreaming"? Is it a struggle to maintain the relationship? To work at a relationship is one thing, but to continuously struggle to maintain a relationship is another. If it's a constant struggle, it may be time to move on. Big-eyed, success-minded people know when to let go.

If you found out that something you'd brought into your home was poisoning you or your family, you would remove it from your home immediately – wouldn't you? Toxic people spread toxins – negativity, harsh criticism, and pessimism. Toxic people have limited vision – narrow eyes. They can always find something wrong, or something to complain about. Just as you would remove the poisons from your home, it's important to remove poisonous people from your life. That becomes especially important when that person is a close relative, someone who has frequent access to you, someone who is more than an innocent bystander in your life.

Unfortunately, sometimes the most toxic people in our lives are the people who are closest to us. They know us best, have known us longest, and know what buttons to push. And they can be our biggest detractors when we attempt to make radical changes in our lives.

ROLL THE STONE AWAY

Sacrificing ourselves for others is something we've all learned to do. Sacrificing for others at the expense of our own well-being is a different story – especially if that person is your mother, father, spouse, or best friend. Many years ago, my minister preached an Easter sermon that addressed this issue.

Entitled *"Roll the Stone Away,"* the essence of the sermon was that whoever is holding you back – whether it is your mother, father, spouse, sister, or brother – is a stone, and you have to "roll the stone away."

In other words, you must find the strength to let go. Failure to rid ourselves of these heavy stones (toxic people) will ultimately result in the stones weighing us down and keeping us from reaching our goals. These stones become a burden and a drain, not adding anything to our lives, but taking time and energy and, if we're not careful, rolling over and crushing our dreams.

When I reflect on relationships and my inner circle, I am reminded of a passage from a book I read once that dealt with the seating charts for our lives.

Who's sitting where in your life? Do the people who are most helpful, who believe in you the most and are the most supportive, have front-row seats, or do the narrow-eyed dream-killers and negative Neds occupy those seats? Did you consciously adopt this seating chart or take what the fates sent your way? Perhaps you need to take a long, hard look at your life and the people around you and rearrange the seating chart of your life.

Remember that you're in the driver's seat, and the people sitting closest to you should be the ones who will help you navigate the rough terrain, those who want to see you reach your destination, the people who can see and support your dreams.

Does that mean that we have to cut off contact with the people in the back seat – the stones? Not at all! It simply means that we need to rearrange the seating chart to ensure that the correct people are seated in the front row in our lives and that the back-seaters have less influence on us.

When building and cultivating your relationships and building your inner circle, ask yourself if the people within your inner-circle bring, have, or offer the following attributes:

> **Intimacy:** Within your circle you need to have people who provide you with closeness, warmth, and acceptance – people with whom you can express your feelings freely without fearing any kind of repercussions, ridicule, or backlash. These are people who love and believe in you unconditionally.

> **Ego-strokes:** People sitting in the front row of your life should make you feel good about yourself. They should help boost your self-esteem and sense of self-worth. With them you feel important, capable, strong, and extra-special.

> **A strong sense of self:** Because these people feel good about themselves it's easy for them to be supportive of you. You'll find that they have hopes and dreams of their own, and their goals and objectives may even be similar to yours. You share ideas, information, and experiences, and can dream together.

Support through thick and thin: The people closest to you should be the people who are there when times are good, and when times are not so good. They should be there to applaud you when you're up and to lift you when you're down. They should be there, standing right beside you, in times of crisis.

Challenges: Some people are challenging to the point of exhaustion – that's not what we mean here. The people in your inner circle, your friends and confidantes, should challenge you to open your eyes wider, to reach higher, to take a leap of faith, to try new things. By the same measure, they should challenge you by encouraging you to think outside the box... by questioning your decisions to help ensure, as much as you can, that you've made the best decision. They should challenge you to be the best that you can be, and never let you settle for less than your best.

Key Points to Remember

People come into our lives for a season, a reason, or a lifetime. Not all relationships are forever. Don't be afraid to let go – to roll away the stones.

☉

Relationships must be nurtured, but more importantly they must be nurturing.

☉

Just say "no" to toxic people. You are in the driver's seat and you don't have to tolerate people who are negative, who undermine your dreams, and who chip away at your self-esteem.

☉

Create an imaginary "velvet rope" around your inner circle. Allow in only those people who love, nourish, challenge, and support you.

☉

Learn to be selfish. Stop sacrificing yourself for others – especially those people who don't have your best interests at heart.

☉

Surround yourself with big eyed people. Spend your valuable time with people who also have hopes, dreams, and aspirations.

> *Believe... that by surrounding yourself with the right people you will achieve lasting and optimum success.*

Think on This: How do you evaluate the quality of your inner circle? What attributes does your inner circle offer? Who do you need to see more of? Less of?

Act on This: Take whatever steps necessary to rearrange the seating chart of your life. Eliminate, or position at a distance, all toxic relationships. Make sure your inner circle aligns with your values, vision, and goals.

Chapter 7:

BE POSITIVE

Keep Your Big Eyes Bright

*A great attitude does much more than turn on the
lights in our worlds; it seems to magically connect us
to all sorts of serendipitous opportunities that
were somehow absent before the change.*
- Earl Nightingale

As we go about writing the drama that is to be our life, how do we weather the storms and turbulent waters? How do we steer through the troubles, disappointments, temptations and opposition to our intentions, the distractions from our focus? How do we keep our big eyes shining and focused on the prize – even when the road is filled with twists and turns?

We do it through the continuous practice of a good mental diet. In other words, we continuously practice having a positive attitude, despite whatever is going on in our life. I define attitude as your state of mind, the way you look at things, or the disposition you transmit to others. *You can see an attitude.* It is expressed before you say a word. Your attitude shows in the way you look, stand, walk or talk.

Your attitude sets the stage for everything that will happen to you in your life. As Keith Harrell states in his book, *Attitude Is Everything*, "A positive attitude is the foundation of a successful life. It is the most valuable asset you can possess." Charles Swindoll wrote: "Attitude is more important than the past, than education, than money, than circumstances, than what people do or say. It's more important than appearance, giftedness, or skill." For many companies, attitude is king. For instance, Southwest Airlines "hires for attitude and trains for skill." To me and many others, attitude is more important than what is on one's resume.

When I think about the role attitude has played in my life, I am reminded of Susan, my first full-time staff member.

I started my workshop and seminar business in 1987. Shortly after going into business, I was awarded a contract to provide training programs to a high-profile federal government agency. About eight months into the contract, I realized I needed an on-site project manager. Immediately I remembered a young lady who had attended one of my workshops. I remembered her because she exuded energy and enthusiasm and was always smiling. I was impressed with her energy level. I tracked her down and recruited her for my company. At that time, Susan didn't have a college degree, nor did she have experience in the training business. Several people with college degrees, even advanced degrees, were interested in the position, but I wanted Susan. Later I was asked, "What made Susan so special?" The reason was quite simple. She had a great personality and an even greater attitude. I figured that with an attitude like hers, I could teach her anything and she could learn anything. I was right! She could and she did.

Some people believe that 1) something outside of us causes a "bad" attitude, and 2) others can cause us to have a bad attitude. Both are false assumptions. Attitudes come from within. They are created, controlled, and influenced by our beliefs –what we are programmed to believe by ourselves or by others. Our attitude comes from our thoughts. And thoughts are induced by our internal dialogue (our self-talk). For most of us, that dialogue is non-stop. The mind is rarely blank. There is always chatter, chatter, chatter. And much of the chatter is negative, destructive, and counterproductive.

> *Attitudes come from within.*

Let's put this to a test. For thirty seconds, sit quietly, close your eyes, and think about absolutely nothing.

Some of you may have been able to block out everything, but probably most of you thought about a dozen different things. You see, the mind is always racing unless you train it to do otherwise.

Regarding the false assumption that others can cause you to have a bad attitude: no one can cause you to have a bad attitude without your permission. No matter your circumstances or what has happened to you in your life, you have complete control over your attitude.

This reminds me of a story I heard many years ago about a little boy and a bully. A different and similar version of this story has been floating around for at least two or more decades. But here is the version I like.

A little boy moved to a new neighborhood. He rode the bus to school. Over the years he had developed the habit of standing up and looking out of the window while riding. On the bus this particular day was a bully. When the little boy stood up, the bully pushed him down in his seat. The little boy stood up again. The bully pushed him down again. The third time the little boy was pushed down, he just sat there smiling. Puzzled, the bully asked, "What are you smiling about?" The little boy responded, "I am standing up inside of myself."

The moral of this story is: We have complete control over our attitude and over the way we respond in any given situation. It's not the stuff that happens to us, it's how we respond to the "stuff" that counts.

You may only be an attitude away from achieving optimum success — from realizing your deepest desires. When things are not going your way, the attitude you adopt is your best defense. Maintaining a positive outlook takes commitment and hard work. Here are some actions that will help you consistently practice maintaining a positive attitude.

SMILE

The smile is your million-dollar asset. You can work miracles with a smile. People simply don't smile enough. Have you ever noticed the look on the faces of people going to and from work? Most look as if they are angry at the world. Have you ever been walking down the street and a total stranger said, "Honey, smile. Things can't be that bad"? Smiling is a way to write your feelings on your face. It communicates that you are friendly, happy, and approachable.

Why is this important? Friendly, happy, approachable people get more opportunities than unfriendly, unhappy, unapproachable people. It's a known fact that you feel better when you smile. Now if these are not enough reasons to smile, think about this: you look better when you smile. Some people think that it's not possible to smile all the time. But by using a technique I refer to as "mouth yoga," you can train yourself to keep a smile on your face. In "mouth yoga," you hold the corners of your mouth turned up in a very slight smile at all times.

Initially when you practice mouth yoga, you might feel a bit strange. But keep practicing. You've heard the saying, "Practice makes perfect." To some extent, that is true. I believe, however, that practice makes permanent. By practicing mouth yoga, you will develop a permanent (perfect) smile. This quote from an unknown source clearly underscores the importance of smiling: "You are never fully dressed without a smile."

BE ENTHUSIASTIC

William James, a noted American philosopher, stated, "You feel the way you act." To feel enthusiastic, you must act enthusiastically. Let your enthusiasm radiate in your eyes, your face, your walk, in the words you use and the thoughts you choose. People who are enthusiastic smile more, walk faster, and use more positive words. Enthusiasm – like a smile – is contagious and it's magic. It's an emotion that can be communicated more easily than words. In the game of life, enthusiasm can mean the difference between winning and losing, the difference between success and failure. Ralph Waldo Emerson wrote: "Nothing was ever achieved without enthusiasm."

AVOID NEGATIVE PEOPLE

You may not be responsible for who sits next to you on a daily basis, but you *are* responsible for who you allow in your inner circle. As I pointed out in Chapter 6, don't deliberately surround yourself with narrow-eyed, gloom and doom (toxic) people. Periodically re-evaluate the quality of your inner circle; those people who occupy a front-row seat in your life. Ask yourself, "Are there 'toxic' relationships in my front row? Do these relationships nourish and nurture me?" If they don't, it may be time to either "let go" or rearrange the seating chart, placing relationships that are not in your best interest in the back seat.

There are some toxic people who, for whatever reason, you may be unable to avoid or place in a back seat. Prior to encountering these people, I've learned to bombard my mind with self-affirming, positive, happy, peaceful thoughts and words. A daily diet of positive words can help you in many stressful and difficult situations.

My final thought on negative people is: Don't walk away from negative people. *RUN! As fast as you can.*

(I encourage you to revisit Chapter 6, Build Relationships, for a review on how to cultivate and nurture a supportive inner circle – the *right* relationships.)

PLAY YOUR WINNERS

Always focus on the positive. For every negative, there is a flip side – a positive or a lesson to be learned. My mother was a master at looking at the flip side. Her personal motto was "I won't complain." No matter what was happening in her life, my mother always looked at it from the positive side. She never, ever complained about anything. She truly lived her personal motto. At her funeral (when she was ninety years old), *I Won't Complain* was one of the funeral songs. To her family, friends, and neighbors, she had developed a reputation for not complaining; for always looking on the bright side.

When I look at my life, at all of the blessings and favors I have and am receiving, I am afraid to complain. Perhaps I got that trait from my mother. I hope that I also inherited her genes for longevity!

When you think you're having it bad, keep everything in the proper perspective. Here is another old story that has been circulating for years. The source is unknown. I don't know whether it's a true story, but it underscores the importance of keeping everything in perspective.

One day a father of a very wealthy family took his son on a trip to the country for the purpose of showing his son how poor people live. They spent a couple of days and nights on the farm of what would be considered a very poor family. On their return from their trip, the father asked his son, "How was the trip?" "It was great, Dad." "Did you see how poor people live?" the father asked. "Oh yeah," said the son. "So tell me, what did you learn from the trip?' asked the father. The son answered, "I saw that we have one dog and they had four. We have a pool that reaches to the middle of our garden and they have a creek that has no end. We have imported lanterns in our garden and they have the stars at night. Our patio reaches to the front yard, while they have the whole horizon. We have a small piece of land to live on and they have fields that go beyond our sight. We have servants who serve us, but they serve others. We buy our food, but they grow theirs. We have walls around our property to protect us; they have friends to protect them." The boy's father was speechless. Then his son added, "Thanks, Dad, for showing me how poor we are."

Isn't perspective a wonderful thing? Makes you wonder what would happen if we all gave thanks for everything we have, instead of worrying about what we don't have.

What are your winners – the positive things that are happening in your life right now? You may have thought of things such as:

"I have a supportive family."

"I have some good friends."

"I have my health."

"I am spiritually anchored."

"I live in a beautiful city."

"I have a roof over my head."

When the going gets tough, play your winners.

WATCH YOUR TALK, THE WORDS YOU USE

Some words and phrases will trigger negative emotions. Examples include "can't," "never," "impossible," "if," or "This will never work."

Let's look at the word *can't*. My mother use to say, "There is no such thing as *can't*. You can do anything you set your mind to do." People use "can't" when they either don't want to do something or don't know how. Rather than explaining or saying no, it's easier to say "I can't." The only legitimate "can't" is something you are physically unable to do. For years I walked around saying, "I can't ride a bike." Then, at age fifty-three (tired of explaining why I couldn't ride a bike), I went out and bought a beautiful red bike and learned to ride it in about two weeks. Another one of my favorites was, "I can't run." Again, tired of coming up with excuses as to why I could not, I decided to give it a try. Not only did I find out that I could run, I could run long distances. At age fifty-eight, I ran my first marathon. And I didn't come in last!

The next time you hear yourself saying that you can't do something, simply ask yourself, "Am I physically unable to do this?" If you're not physically unable to do it, then change the "I can't" to "I don't want to" or "I choose not to."

Another word that can trigger negative emotions is "try." Once upon a time, my niece began most of her responses to requests with, "I'll try." I would respond, "I don't want you to try, I want you to do it." The word "try" implies that there is the possibility of failure, and not only are you preparing for it, you're accepting it. Yoda said, "Try not. Do, or do not. There is no try."

Just as it is important to watch the words you use, it's equally important to monitor your thoughts. Over the years a great deal has been written and said about the power of thought. All the greatest teachers, philosophers, psychologists, and historians in the entire history of the world agree that "we become what we think." For example, Marcus Aurelius, a second century Roman emperor, stated, "A man's life is what his thoughts make of it. Change your thoughts, change your life." The Bible states, "As a man thinkest in his heart, so is he."

I once heard a minister say, "If bad things are always happening in your life, ask yourself, "Is my thinking stinking?" It probably is. Stinking thinking attracts stinking results. If you want to change the results, change your thoughts. You change your thoughts by simply changing your internal dialogue (your self-talk).

DISPLAY A POSITIVE ATTITUDE TOWARD OTHERS

Be interested in others. Display the attitude you want to attract. And look for the good in others.

The following story is old, but the message is the same today as it was yesterday. An old man would sit outside the walls of the ancient city where he lived. Every day he would sit and tell stories to the children. One day he was approached by a stranger who stated that he was thinking about moving to the city and wanted to know the kind of people living there. The old man replied, "What kind of people live in the city you are from?" The stranger replied, "The people in my city are unkind, selfish, cheat, steal, and lie. I am leaving because of the undesirable people who live there." The old man responded, "That is exactly the kind of people you will find in this city." Disappointed, the stranger walked away. A short time later, another stranger, with the same question, approached the old man. The old man's response was the same: "What kind of people live in the city you are from?" The stranger replied, "The people in my city are friendly, helpful, kind, and charitable. I really hate to leave." The old man responded, "That is exactly the kind of people you will find in this city. Welcome." The children, who had observed both exchanges, sat in silence. Finally, one of them approached the old man and asked, "Why, sir, didn't you tell those men the truth?" The old man explained, "I did tell the truth. You see, no matter where you go or what you do, you will find in other people exactly what you are looking for. *If you search for the good, you will find it; but if you look for the bad that is what you will undoubtedly see.*"

So make life easier – always look for the good. Expect the best from others. People will normally live up or down to your expectations.

Expect the best from others.
People will normally live up or down to your expectations.

It's also important that you speak well of others. Another little tidbit about my mother – in all of my years, I never heard her say an unkind word about anyone. And I can't even imagine anyone saying an unkind word about her.

The next time you feel compelled to utter a negative word or have a negative thought about someone, just remember the saying, "What goes around comes around." In other words, you get back what you give out – sooner or later.

Herm Albright is credited with the statement, "A positive attitude may not solve all of your problems but it will annoy enough people to make it worth the effort."

Key Points to Remember

A positive mental diet helps you weather the storms of life.

❂

Attitude sets the stage for everything that will happen to you in your life. It's the foundation of a successful life.

❂

No matter what's going on in your life, you always have complete control over your attitude.

❂

A smile is your million-dollar asset. You can work miracles with a smile.

❂

Enthusiasm, like a smile, is contagious. It can mean the difference between winning and losing.

❂

Watch the company you keep; avoid negative people.

❂

Focus on what you have, not what you don't have.

❂

Rid your vocabulary of words that trigger negative emotions – *can't, if, never, try.*

❂

You will find in other people exactly what you're looking for. So make your life easy. Always look for the good.

> *Believe... that a positive mental attitude is the best defense against adversity.*

Think on This: Which song best describes your attitude? In the face of adversity and disappointments, will your big eyes continue to be bright?

Act on This: Practice "mouth yoga." Make an attitude adjustment. Whenever you have a critical thought about someone, focus on their best qualities instead. Whenever you catch yourself complaining about your life, count your blessings. Whenever you think or say "I can't," correct yourself and say, "I don't know how to..." or "I choose not to."

Chapter 8:
PRACTICE SELF-CARE
To Thine Own Big Eyes Be Good

Self-preservation is the first law of nature.
- Samuel Butler

*There's no better way to energize your body, mind,
and spirit than by taking care of yourself.*
- Stephanie Tourles, Author, *50 Ways to Pamper Yourself*

A book about how to expand your vision to achieve optimum success wouldn't be complete if I didn't devote space to taking care of yourself, or self-care. To live abundantly, you must make fitness, health, and wellness your top priorities. *Without optimum health, you'll never experience optimum success.*

There are some myths surrounding the notion of self-care, especially when it's viewed as a way of life that encourages us to put ourselves first. Many people, especially women, are uncomfortable with the notion of putting themselves first. We're often raised to believe that we should put our spouse's, children's, or elderly parents' needs before our own. But how can we take care of others if we haven't taken care of ourselves, and are less than we need to be physically, mentally, spiritually, and yes, financially?

You can't help someone else if you can't help yourself! That's why it's of the utmost importance to take care of self, first. A great example of the importance of putting ourselves first is the set of instructions we receive when traveling by plane. As the airplane is preparing for takeoff, the flight attendant gives instructions on how to use the oxygen mask. We are told that if we are traveling with a small child to put our oxygen mask on first, then the child's. You can't help the child if you've passed out from a lack of oxygen. In fact, you're likely to do both yourself and the child more harm than good if you don't take care of yourself first in this scenario.

Taking care of ourselves is the responsible thing to do! Self-care is defined in many ways. Some simply define it as nurturing one's self. My definition takes it a few steps further to include the following:

- Having balance in our lives

- Taking or making time to rejuvenate ourselves

- Taking or making the time to talk to ourselves, to build up and inspire ourselves, to congratulate ourselves on our successes and forgive ourselves for our mistakes

- Taking care of our minds, bodies, and spirits – by eating right, exercising, and spending quiet time with ourselves

- Incorporating into our daily lives behaviors that help us be the best we can be

- Putting ourselves first

The following are some actions you can start to practice today to help you to not only achieve your goals, but also to ensure that you're mentally, physically, and spiritually able to enjoy them once you've achieved them. *Remember, nothing has a greater impact on our ability to achieve lasting success than what we do to and for ourselves, starting today!*

HEALTH IS WEALTH

Exercise is important, period! Research has consistently shown that exercise is the best weapon against age-related diseases and disabilities.

Many years ago a friend made a major career change, from an administrative position in the space industry to the health care industry, specializing in the field of aging. At age forty-six, she went back to school so she could achieve her life-long dream of working with the elderly. Sometimes she was overwhelmed by the health challenges of many of her clients. Once she remarked that many of those challenges resulted from the poor health and lifestyle choices her clients had made – consciously or unconsciously – twenty, thirty, or forty years ago. Many people not only had limited financial resources, but overwhelming health problems. It was a wake-up call for both of us.

All the money and success in the world can't buy health. It may get you better doctors but there's only so much they can do if you've squandered your health.

To minimize age-related health challenges, some form of physical activity or exercise should be incorporated in our daily lives.

MAKE WISER FOOD CHOICES

Making wiser food choices is one of the simplest things we can do for ourselves today to guarantee a more fulfilling tomorrow and optimum success. This doesn't mean that we must adhere to a strict diet, nor does it mean that we can never indulge in those foods we sometimes crave. It does mean, however, that we should and can incorporate lower-calorie, more nutritious foods into our daily diets.

And it means that daily run through a fast-food drive-thru must become a thing of the past. If you're pressed for time and decide to use the drive-thru, vow to order a salad instead of a burger and fries. Most of the fast food establishments now make it easier to make wiser food choices by offering a variety of salads, low-cal dressings, fruit, and bottled water.

Some small changes you can make that are wiser food choices are:

- Drink plenty of water. It helps flush toxins out of the body, helps with digestion, and is the only thing we can put into our bodies that has no calories but does offer great benefits.

- Eat more fruit, whole grains, and vegetables.

- Choose foods that are low in saturated fat and cholesterol.

- Avoid foods containing trans-fats.

- Avoid refined flour and sugars.

- Drink alcohol in moderation, if at all.

If you are really serious about developing healthy eating habits, you may want to engage the services of a nutritionist. In working with a nutritionist, it's important to: 1) Know what you want to accomplish (your goal), and 2) feel comfortable with the relationship. Eating a healthy diet is like exercising. When you make it a daily habit, it will come as naturally to you as brushing your teeth.

LEARN TO RELAX

Relaxing means different things to different people. For some people, relaxing means being in a self-induced state in which the mind and body are calm, quiet, and at rest. Approaches to getting into such a state may include meditation, prayer, visualization exercises, progressive muscle relaxation, or deep breathing. For others, it means doing things they enjoy, such as running, walking, biking, gardening, watching movies, reading, or simply doing nothing. I say whatever floats your boat.

Whatever mode of relaxation you choose, remember that it's important to relax. Take time away from the hustle and bustle of the world to be alone with your thoughts. Take time to plan, to dream, and to recharge your batteries. And remember to be selfish – shut off the phone, shut off the world. Be consistent, be good to yourself, and take time to relax.

PRACTICE GOOD TIME MANAGEMENT

We all get the same amount of time each week – 168 hours – to do everything that we need and want to do. Some people accomplish a great deal in those 168 hours, while others get little done. Some people complain about not having enough time while others simply make the best use of the time they have. People who accomplish everything they need and want to do have learned the fine art of time management.

Time management is really self-management. We can't manage time; we can only manage ourselves. To manage ourselves means making the best use of the time we have. There is no such thing as the lack of time. We all have time to do whatever we really want to do. It all boils down to our priorities – deciding on those activities that will yield the best results and move us closer to attaining our goals.

Many people use the ABC method of setting priorities. A's are those things you *must* do or suffer critical consequences; B's are those things you *should* do. The "should do's" are generally activities that are high on others' list of priorities. And C's are those things that are *nice* to do. Most of us spend much of our time on nice-to-do's – those activities that keep us busy but add little to our overall health, wealth, or well-being.

When developing a good time management system, we must keep in mind that only 20% of what we do is critical to our success. The challenge is attempting to accurately identify those critical elements. Most people can't identify the critical elements – those activities that will ensure success.

Here are some time management tips that I find helpful.

➤ **Begin each day with something you want to accomplish.** To do this, you must have goals and a plan. For example, at the beginning of each day, I decide on at least one thing I will accomplish. This one thing is always related, directly or indirectly, to one of my goals. One of my major goals relates to health and wellness. Therefore, each day I plan on engaging in at least one activity to support this goal.

➤ **Use a "to do" list.** The "to do" list is an important time management tool. This is *not* a list of those activities you plan to do in life. It includes only those things you plan to do that day. This is why it's sometimes referred to as a daily to-do list. Some people make the list the night before, while others make the list first thing in the morning. The list is to include not only those critical activities you need to do for others (your children, spouse, bosses, parents, etc.), but those activities you need to do to take better care of yourself. When making your list, keep in mind that only 20% of what you do is critical to your success. A to-do list will help you keep track of daily goals and can serve as a self-pat on the back at the end of the day when you realize how productive you've been and how well you stuck to your plans.

⊚ **Eliminate time-wasters and time-wasting habits.** A time-waster is any activity that keeps you from moving toward your goals. They devour our time but add nothing of substance to our lives. For many of us, time-wasters include unnecessary phone conversations, drop-in visitors, shopping, television, procrastination, and the inability to say no. Ultimately, only you can decide what your time-wasters are. You should also determine if you have any habits or daily practices that are time-wasters. These can include tangibles, things like sitting on the couch watching television when you should be doing something else, and intangibles, like spending time worrying and complaining. Worrying and complaining are two of the biggest time bandits known to humankind.

⊚ **Be conscious of your actions.** As you go through the day remain conscious of your actions – what you're doing and why you're doing it. Ask yourself if what you're doing at any given moment is something that will move you closer to your goals and dreams. Is what you're doing an "A" or a "C," and is there something else you could and should be doing at that very moment that's more beneficial to your success – in the short run or in the long run?

The more you practice being conscious of what you're doing throughout the day, the more it will become second nature and the more you'll find yourself on track – that is, eliminating the time-wasters and scheduling your day in a way that enables you to accomplish more and more of the things that will bring you closer to achieving your goals.

⊙ **Avoid the perfection trap.** In the Malaysian Culture, there is a saying: "Only the gods are considered capable of producing anything perfect. Whenever something is made, a flaw is left on purpose so the gods will not be offended."

Contrary to what many people think, perfectionism, which I define as paying attention to unnecessary details, is not a virtue. Striving for perfection is a personality flaw, a major time-waster, and a set-up for disappointment. Do the best you can and move on – let your best be good enough. Some things don't need to be done perfectly. They just need to be done.

⊙ **Learn to say no.** "No" is not a bad word. Saying "no" doesn't make you a bad person. Sometimes saying no to others means saying yes to ourselves, and to what we really want to achieve in our lives. Staying focused often means saying "no" to the people and other distractions that would pull you off course. Learning to say "no" is about learning to set boundaries and priorities for our lives.

Because others may not know about your goals, may not understand them, or may not believe in or respect what you're trying to accomplish, it's up to you to say no to the things and people that stand between you and your goals.

For many people the word "no" is the hardest word in the English language. We can master the ability to say no by recognizing that we have a right, and sometimes a need, to say "no," and mean it.

MAKE THANKFULNESS A HABIT

Meister Eckhardt stated, "If the only prayer you ever say in your entire life is thank you, it will be enough."

There will always be people who have more than you have. There will always be people who have less than you. The key is to be thankful for what you have and where you are in life. When we start to compare ourselves to others, we start to feel inadequate.

Just because someone is blessed with material possessions doesn't mean that person is happy. All the money in the world isn't worth anything if you're alone, unhappy, and have no one to share it with.

Be thankful for everything, great or small. Make it a habit to thank people for little things, even when they don't expect it. When I think about gratitude, I often think about my mother, who exemplified gratitude in its humblest and simplest form, and who taught me the true spirit of gratitude.

When my oldest brother passed away he left my mother a modest sum of money. We asked her what she was going to spend it on. Her reply: "I already have everything I want. My children are all grown, I have a decent house to live in, and I am in good health for an eighty-seven-year-old. As long as I have family, friends, and faith, then I'm grateful." My mother's words remind me to take a moment each day to be grateful for good health, a sound body and mind, for family and friends, and for my daily bread – to not bemoan what I don't have, but to be grateful for the things I do have.

USE HUMOR TO LIGHTEN YOUR EMOTIONAL LOAD

Humor is a powerful tonic. People who can laugh at themselves are healthier, happier, and live longer, more fulfilling lives. They are also much more resilient. I associate humor with lightness, joy, and laughter. Studies have shown that people who use humor on a daily basis were ranked as outstanding twice as often as those who don't. Further, they earn more money.

Like any skill, humor can be learned. People can be taught to lighten up. Of course, keep in mind that what is funny to one person may not be funny to another. Here are a few tips for learning to lighten up:

- Maintain a log of funny stories (especially your own) and jokes.

- Although humor doesn't mean telling jokes, jokes can help wake up your humor gene.

- Watch comedies and read funny books.

- Use Post-It notes to remind yourself to not take things so seriously; remind yourself to laugh more often.

- Daily affirm your ability to see the humor in many situations, even those that are serious.

- Include some funny people in your inner circle.

- Take a humor class or workshop.

- Use pin-up cartoons or sayings that tickle your funnybone.

Key Points to Remember

Self-preservation is the first law of nature. To live abundantly, you must make fitness, health, and wellness your top priorities.

❧

Make wise food choices. Small steps can lead to better health. Plan meals, snack on fruits and vegetables, and reduce consumption of fast foods and high-sodium packaged meals.

❧

Learn to relax. Be a little selfish – carve out some "me" time each day. Use this time to think, to recharge your batteries, read, or do nothing at all.

❧

Learn to manage your self (time) wisely. We can't manage time; we can only manage ourselves.

❧

Stop striving for perfection. Remember that when you've done your best, it's the best you can do. Perfection is an impossible, unrealistic, and self-defeating goal.

❧

Learn to say no. Saying "no" doesn't make you a bad person, and can, in fact, make you a better person.

❧

Be grateful. Stop worrying and complaining about what you don't have, and be thankful for what you do have. There will always be people with more, and with less, than you. See your blessings glass as half full, rather than half empty.

☉

Laugh more. You will be healthier, happier, and you will live longer.

Believe...that you can achieve much more when you take good care of yourself first and foremost.

Think on This: What can you start doing today to take better care of yourself (physically, mentally, and emotionally)? What can you do to bring more balance into your life?

Act on This: List those things here. Now do them – every day.

Chapter 9:
MIND YOUR MONEY

Open Your Big Eyes to Wealthfulness

Expose yourself constantly to wealthful ideas –
think prosperity, think substance, think affluence.

- Eric Butterworth

Never spend your money before you have it.

- Thomas Jefferson

Some may think that it's crass to talk about money in a book where so much of the message has to do with inner satisfaction, self-esteem, and creative expression. Just as these things are crucial to achieving lasting and optimum success – in business and in life – so is fiscal responsibility.

So how can I *not* talk about money? Surveys have consistently shown that, for many people, success is in some way – directly or indirectly – related to having enough money to meet basic needs or to fulfill your life purpose. You'll need financial support, whether you want to study, start a business, travel, or devote your life to helping others.

For example, Eric Butterworth, who coined the word wealthfulness, points out in his book *Spiritual Economics* that "Money supported Albert Schweitzer in the steaming jungles of Africa where he labored unselfishly for the natives. Gandhi, in his extreme poverty, going about the land of India, with his loin cloth and a little spinning wheel, giving the image of abject poverty, required a lot of money to care for him and his entourage." One of Gandhi's followers is credited with the statement, "It takes an awful lot of money to keep Gandhi living in poverty."

The bottom line is: no matter how you define success or what you're doing in your life or plan to do with your life, *money matters*. So widen you eyes and reshape your attitude about money. There is little likelihood that you will achieve lasting and optimum success without taking a positive and creative approach to handling your finances. The inability to mind your money impacts every aspect of your life – on and off the job. Yes, *money matters*!

MONEY MATTERS!

How often have you heard or even said, "Money doesn't matter"? How do we treat things that matter? And how do we treat things that don't matter?

When things matter, we pay attention to them. We treat them with care; we are mindful of what we do with them; we are gentle with them; and we learn about them. This is the attitude we need to have with our money if we want it to be there for us – when we need it most.

On the other hand, when things don't matter, we are frivolous with them. At times, we may even throw them away without a second thought. That is how some of us treat money. On a subconscious level, I have always known that money matters. Yet there were times when I had that "money doesn't matter" attitude.

In college, I majored in Business Administration. During my sophomore year, I had a part-time bookkeeping and office assistant job, working for one of my business professors. I worked every other Saturday in his home office. One Saturday, after several months, he told me that I deserved a raise. He asked me how much I thought I should get. I responded, "It really doesn't matter. Money doesn't mean that much to me." For the next thirty minutes, I got a stern lecture on the fact that "money matters" and "should mean something to me." Almost forty years later, I am still learning just how much money matters.

Have you noticed that people are somewhat reluctant to talk about money? There seems to be a taboo associated with it. It's just not politically correct to talk about it.

I believe part of that reluctance stems from those early childhood messages we received, messages such as:

- ❧ "It is easier for a camel to go through the eye of a needle than it is for a rich man to enter the Kingdom of heaven."

141

- "Money isn't everything."

- "Money can't buy happiness."

- "Money is the root of all evil."

A once-famous televangelist used to say that "the lack of money is the root of all evil." People who have money don't talk about it for fear of sounding gauche or tacky. People who don't have it don't talk about it for fear of being looked down on.

But we as a society should be talking about money. With Americans' savings at an all-time low and debt at an all-time high, I think we need to start talking about money a whole lot more. Discussions about money should be taking place in the boardroom, the bedroom, and around the dinner table, where our children can start to learn the importance of fiscal responsibility.

Some people understand the importance and power of money intrinsically. Others have to work a little harder to understand it. My mother understood the power of money. My older sister used to say that my mother could squeeze a dollar out of a dime. The irony is that my mother, who had no formal education, never made or had much money, but kept up burial insurance policies on all of her children and my father, and also left each of us a small inheritance and enough money to cover the costs of her funeral.

I learned about saving for a rainy day from her. No matter how little she earned, she always managed to save. She never used the words *focused, determined,* or *goal-oriented,* but she was all of these things and more.

I was also fortunate enough to marry a man who was a devotee of the "save for a rainy day" theory. And he could have easily been the founding president of the "pay yourself first society," because without fail, he made sure that our savings account was first in line to be paid on payday.

Because we created a savings and investment plan and stuck to it, we eventually had a cushion that enabled us to reach other goals, including purchasing a rental property, taking a vacation each year, and enabling me to start my training and consulting company.

I learned many lessons from both my mother and my ex-husband about the power of money. Other lessons I learned on my own, some the hard way. But I learned them nonetheless. Here are some of the things I learned about money.

> *Money Matters!*

RESPECT THE POWER OF MONEY

Money is a powerful tool. Is yours working for you? Handling your money wisely can make your life better; misusing your monetary resources can make your life miserable. One of the things people are stressed about most is money, or the lack thereof. A study published in 2005 found that one in four U.S.

workers is "seriously financially distressed." This, ultimately, affects job performance and productivity. Money problems can also destroy relationships and cause sleepless nights and other hardship. Respecting money doesn't mean worshiping it, but simply means that you should pay attention to where your money goes, how you spend it, and what you spend it on. Many people can tell you how much they make an hour, a day, a week, and annually, but can't tell you where the money goes. Take care of your money so it will last to take care of you and allow you to do the things that are important to you.

PAY YOURSELF FIRST

This is one of the best and most fruitful lessons I've learned about money. The easiest and fastest way to achieve your financial goals is by making a commitment to save a certain percentage of your income. Many people think they should pay all of their bills first, and if there's anything left, pay themselves.

But as the cost of living continues to rise and salaries fail to keep pace, more and more people find that there's little or nothing left. Nonetheless, paying yourself first may be easier than you think. Does the organization you work for offer direct deposit? If so, take advantage of that program and have your pay deposited directly into your bank account. Many programs will let you put money into more than one account, so you can put some money into your checking account and some into your savings account. The money that goes into your savings account comes off the top and you never have to worry about moving the money from one account to the other, getting to the bank to make a deposit, or being ambushed by a shoe sale on your way to the bank. Another simple way to pay yourself is to enroll in your company's 401k program. Not only does this ensure that you pay yourself first, but because most companies have a matching funds program, you're rewarded for paying yourself.

> *Be good to yourself – pay yourself first.*

SAVE FOR OPPORTUNITIES

Change the way you think about saving. The cliché "save for a rainy day" has been around for decades. But I say, "save for opportunities." While it's important to "save for a rainy day" or those unexpected emergencies, it's equally important that you "save for opportunities"– the unpredictable openings God provides when you find your purpose and set goals. When you "save for opportunities," you not only have the means to handle the curveballs that life throws your way, you'll also have the resources to take advantage of positive opportunities that may occasionally unfold. To only save for a rainy day implies a "you expect bad things to happen," or a reactive, consciousness, while saving for opportunity implies a proactive consciousness. Expect good things to happen! Save for opportunities not just emergencies.

KNOW WHERE YOUR MONEY GOES

Has anyone ever said to you: "I don't know where my money goes"? Have you ever been the one saying "I don't know where my money goes"? People who say that usually don't have a lot of money because they let it slip through their fingers. People who have serious money know where their money goes, usually down to the penny. That's because they have their mind on their money, and their money on their mind. Their eyes are open wide to wealthfulness. Be conscious of how much you spend, where you spend, and how you spend.

Do you plan your spending, or are you an impulsive spender? Do you go to the mall saying that you're going to look, only to find yourself leaving the mall a few hundred dollars less rich? Or worse, with your credit card balance ever rising? Set limits on yourself and don't allow yourself to spend more than that set limit. Help yourself by:

- Creating a budget and sticking to it.

- Recording every purchase in a notebook in order to see exactly where and how you're spending your money. Reviewing it at the end of each day can help you determine where you can cut spending and save more.

- Leaving your debit card and checkbook at home when going to the mall. This will cut down on impulse spending and also give you time to consider if you really need or want the item that caught your fancy.

- 👁 Using your ATM card as little as possible. ATMs are a necessary evil, but an evil nonetheless. There's an ATM machine on practically every corner. They encourage and enable us to spend more money than we should, and it costs money to use an ATM at a bank where you don't have an account.

USE CREDIT WISELY

Credit is important, but too often people abuse and misuse it. When using credit cards make sure that you don't take on more than you can handle; that you pay your credit card bill on time and, to the extent possible, pay outstanding balances in full or within ninety days. This is especially important if you use your credit card, as I do, to earn reward points or to keep track of all your purchases.

Before making a credit card purchase, ask yourself if the item you want to purchase is something you need, or simply want. If it's something you need, determine if there's a less expensive item you can purchase instead.

If the item is a want rather than a need, why not save for it so you can pay cash or pay the outstanding credit card balance in full? Not only will it cost you less – no interest – you'll also feel good that you were able to set and reach your savings goal.

There is more to using credit wisely than just paying bills on time and not overusing credit.

How often have you been shopping and saw an advertisement that said: "Open an account today and receive 10 percent off"? Or when you stepped up to the counter to pay for your purchase with cash or a check or a major credit card, the sales clerk looked at you, smiled, and said, "Would you like to save ten percent by opening up a store credit card account? It will only take a few minutes."

Just say no. Many times, what sounds like a good deal isn't so good in the long run. Each time you open a new account, it impacts your credit score – the number lenders use to make decisions regarding your ability to repay a debt. Your credit score is a snapshot of your credit risk at a given point in time. Scores are ranked from 300 to 850. A low credit score can mean higher interest rates on homes and cars, and higher car insurance premiums. Some employers even use credit scores to determine your ability to succeed in your job; and landlords may use the scores to determine your desirability as a tenant. So to that ten percent discount for opening a store credit account, *just say no.*

KEEP YOUR DEBT LOAD LIGHT

There's a reason it's called a debt load. Excessive debt can hinder your ability to achieve lasting and optimum success. It can weigh you down like an anchor around your neck. Being unable to pay your bills or meet your financial obligations leads to a host of problems, not the least of which are depression, damage to your self-esteem, and making you feel like a failure. Debt is easy to get into – hard to get out of.

LEARN ABOUT MONEY

Learning about money means knowing how to spend it, save it, invest it, and grow it. It also means understanding terms such as assets, liabilities, net worth, and cash flow. An asset is what you own. A liability is what you owe. You find your net worth by subtracting your assets from your liabilities. Cash flow refers to the amount of money you have coming in (income) and going out (expenses).

Although assets are generally described as what you own, *everything you own is not an asset.* I tend to think of assets as those things you own that increase in value. Items such as clothes, furniture (unless it is an antique or a valuable work of art), and cars do not increase in value. Therefore they're not real assets.

Learning about money also means having some understanding of investment vehicles and terms, such as stocks, bonds, mutual funds, money market accounts, annuities, diversification, and asset allocation.

The more you understand the language of money and other financial matters, the easier it is to widen your big eyes to wealthfulness and mind your money. There are a host of resources available to help you learn about money and money management, including workshops, seminars, books, websites, magazine and newspaper articles, and cable networks devoted to providing information about money.

> *There are so many resources available to help you learn to manage your money that the "I didn't know" excuse just doesn't hold water anymore!*

SEEK HELP

Minding your money also means managing your money. Some people are adept at managing their own money; others need help. If you think that you don't have the time or enough knowledge or confidence to manage your own money, here is a piece of critical advice: *Seek help, but don't blindly turn over the management of your money to another person.*

There are stories on top of stories about people who thought they had a lot of money but left the management of that money to others and didn't practice good oversight. In other words, they didn't "mind" their money. One day they woke up to find that their accountant or business manager had stolen or misappropriated their money. Or they found out that the person they trusted, in some instances a financial advisor, had made some investment decisions that were in his or her best interest, instead of theirs.

If you plan to use the services of a financial advisor, it's still your responsibility to mind your money. And it's critical that you have some basic understanding of the language of money and know what to look for when selecting an advisor.

In deciding to use an advisor, beware of the following:

◉ **The financial planning field is poorly regulated.** Literally *anyone* can have business cards printed up calling themselves a financial planner, advisor, or consultant. Many unsuspecting people have been taken advantage of by so-called financial advisors or financial planners.

◉ **Don't rely on recommendations from your friends.** Unless your friends are legitimately educated about money and investing, they are not your best referral sources. Think about it. How can they refer you to someone when they have never used an advisor and if they have an advisor, don't know how he or she is being paid or even understand their own portfolio?

◉ **Use due diligence when selecting a financial planner.** Using due diligence means learning as much as you can about the person and the organization you are trusting with your money, starting with his or her credentials – experience and qualifications. My ex-husband had a saying: "Never hire someone who is broke to manage your money. If he can't manage his own, how in the world is he going to manage yours?"

Since the financial planning field is poorly regulated, look for an advisor who holds a financial planning designation. Although there are several, the most widely used is the Certified Financial Planning ® (CFP) designation.

According to the CFP website, there are approximately 65,000 CFPs worldwide. A CFP has met stringent educational and experience requirements, agreed to abide by a code of ethics, and passed a national exam administered by the CFP Board of Standards covering these topics: insurance, investments, income taxes, retirement planning, and estate planning.

Many financial advisors are not CFPs. They are salespeople who sell certain products and services.

Even if you have a planner who has the CFP designation, you must still use due diligence. Check them out, monitor your portfolio, and ask questions when you don't understand.

☛ **Don't just sign your name where the arrow is pointed**. Read everything, especially the small print. When it's something you don't understand, ask questions. When it comes to your money, there are no stupid questions.

Not minding your money can cost you – big time.

Key Points to Remember

Be mindful that what you are doing with your money matters.

👁

Respect your money by paying attention to where it goes, how you spend it, and what you spend it on.

👁

Be good to yourself – pay yourself first.

👁

Put aside something for unexpected opportunities.

👁

Use credit wisely. Strive to pay outstanding credit card balances in full.

👁

Just say "no" to that offer of a 10 percent discount for opening up a new credit account.

👁

Keep your debt load light. Excessive debt can hinder your ability to achieve optimum success.

👁

Use the myriad of resources available to help you understand and better manage your money.

👁

Not minding your money can cost you – big time.

Believe…that money matters, is a key component, and can make all the difference in whether or not you're able to fully enjoy the life you've worked hard to make for yourself.

Think on This: What can you start doing today to mind your money?

Act on This: List those things you can start doing today to mind your money. Now start doing them.

Chapter 10:
GIVE BACK

Shine Your Big Eyes on Others

From those to whom much is given, much is expected.

\- Luke 12:48

Think of giving not as a duty but as a privilege.

\- John D. Rockefeller, Jr.

Just as a book on achieving lasting and optimum success would be incomplete without addressing the issues of health and wealth, so would a book that didn't speak to the importance of giving back – shining your big eyes on others. Giving is one of the oldest success principles known to humankind. Catherine Ponder, author of *The Dynamic Laws of Prosperity*, refers to giving as the ancient law of prosperity.

From early childhood I was surrounded by examples of people who gave and gave – whether they had a little or a lot. And most had a little. My greatest role model and mentor was Ms. Arcenia, a very spiritual and kind woman who lived in my neighborhood. In my eyes and the eyes of many of the neighborhood children, Ms. Arcenia was a huge success. She exemplified bigness, which we labeled as success. For instance, she drove a big car, lived in a big house surrounded by land and trees, wore big hats, and worked in a big grocery store instead of as a domestic worker or field hand like most of the other adults I came in contact with. Everyone, including my parents, liked, admired, and respected Ms. Arcenia.

I later learned, however, that our parents had other reasons for admiring her. They admired her because of her capacity to love, to forgive, and to give of herself, her time, and her money. She took a special interest in several children in the neighborhood, especially me. Though childless, she often referred to us as her children. And she supported us as if we were. How did she support us? First and foremost, she did it with her time. Every Sunday morning she would drive through the neighborhood rounding us all up for Sunday school, whether we wanted to go or not. It was not an option. Thanks to Ms. Arcenia, we often spent the entire day at church. Our parents didn't object because they bought into the "it takes a village to raise a child" viewpoint.

Not only did she support us with her time, she did it with her money. She made sure I had a part-time job during the school year – cleaning her house and running errands for her elderly parents while driving her big shiny car – and she paid for my first year of college. Once I overheard someone say to her, "You're always giving to those children; when they grow up they're going to forget you." She responded, "They're not going to forget me. And I do it because I want to." Then she quoted this scripture, which has always stuck with me: "From those to whom much is given, much is expected."

As I got older, I realized that Ms. Arcenia really didn't have *that* much. The car, house, hats, and even the grocery store were not *that* big. They all just seemed so big because what she had, she gave freely. She shined her big eyes on others joyfully. Until the day she departed this earthly world, she embodied the spirit of giving as did my mother, who thought it sacrilegious to not give to your church, whether you attended regularly or not. Even while we were away in college, she faithfully paid our church dues. I think she thought it would give us some added protection.

Why give? We've all heard the saying, "The more you give, the more you'll receive." While that's true, it is not the real reason for giving. You give because it's the *right* thing to do. Albert Einstein stated, "It is every man's obligation to put back into the world at least the equivalent of what he takes out." And Maya Angelou stated, "I have found that among its other benefits, giving benefits the soul of the giver." Giving does make you feel good. At least it does me.

On a subconscious level and, for some, a conscious level, we know the importance and the benefits of giving back. Yet, I am sometime amazed at the number of people who blatantly and unashamedly live for themselves, giving neither time nor money. A *USA Today* poll asked people why they didn't give more of their time and money. Reasons given were:

- They didn't think their donation would be put to good use.

- They didn't have time to participate.

- They had no excess income to give.

- Family commitments consumed their extra time.

Right now you may be having similar thoughts. But I challenge you to look deeper. Is this really the reason? If you really don't have the time or money, then give in other ways: clothes you no longer wear, lunch, a home-cooked meal, a smile, a hug, a kind word, or a helping hand.

People who desire optimum success look for opportunities to shine their big eyes on others, even if it means there is no tax deduction allowed. Don't always allow the Internal Revenue Service (IRS) to dictate your giving strategy. Also don't always expect something in return. Give freely, give joyfully, and give often.

To establish the habit of shining your big eyes on others, here are some tips:

- **Decide.** Make a commitment today to start giving – your time, your money, or both.

- **Identify.** If you don't already have one, identify an organization that could benefit from your experiences or could use some financial support.

◉ **Budget.** If your goal is to give money, set up a "giving" jar. Fund your jar weekly, monthly, or quarterly – whatever works best for you.

◉ **Cultivate relationships.** Start hanging out with people who are known for volunteerism and for their generosity.

◉ **Be grateful.** Develop an attitude of gratitude.

◉ **Teach.** Make giving a family affair. Teach your children to give joyfully. Encourage them to engage in community service projects.

◉ **Give joyfully.** Give expecting nothing in return. Don't always expect to be paid for what you give or for what you do. In the end, it all comes back.

Key Points to Remember

Let your big eyes shine on others by giving back.

👁

Giving is the oldest success principle known to humankind.

👁

From those to whom much is given, much is expected.

👁

Giving benefits the soul.

👁

Look for opportunities to give.

👁

Give expecting nothing in return. Don't always expect to get paid for what you give or for what you do.

> *Believe...that giving is the right thing to do. Then do it!*

Think on This: Why don't you give more of your time and money? Which organizations could benefit from your experiences or could use some financial support?

Act on This: Take action today to shine your big eyes on that organization. Develop a giving strategy. Share your strategy with a family member or friend. Do it ... now!

BIG EYES, BIG EYEDEAS

Putting It All Together

Success often comes to those who have the aptitude
to see way down the road.

- J. Laing Burns, Jr.

This book isn't just about achieving success; it's about achieving optimum success. You may be wondering, "What's the difference?" While success is personal and means different things to different people, optimum success takes your personal definition, whatever that might be, to another level. Optimum implies *best, highest, unequaled,* or *unmatched.* My charge to you is this: take your definition of success to the highest level possible. To get to that highest level, I sincerely believe that it's important that we apply the "Big Eyes" approach to every aspect of our lives, inner and outer – mental, emotional, physical, financial, and spiritual. In this book, I have given you a complete recipe for doing just that. I have provided you with simple, easy-to-implement "how-to" strategies that will help you to achieve excellence in every area of your life. Throughout the book, I have challenged you to *think* and *act.*

When I think of people who have used this approach, I immediately think of my friend, mentor, and Master Mind partner, Erieka. For Erieka, achieving optimum success didn't just happen nor was it an overnight feat. She mapped out a plan and worked her plan. Along the way, she had wilderness experiences that could have broken her focus, her faith, and her spirit. But they didn't because she had a clear vision and a compelling purpose. And she viewed those wilderness experiences as lessons she was to learn as she moved toward what was hers by divine right.

Erieka's story clearly validates the strategies set forth in the preceding chapters.

When I met her in the late eighties, she had already decided that optimum success was her destiny. At that time, what struck me most was her level of confidence in herself, as well as in me. She always felt that I would go on to do great things. She had faith in me even when I doubted myself. She often referred to me as a "GG"– one of God's Girls. In a soft voice and with a serious look on her face, she would say, "All of God's children are special, but you're extra-special. And you're a money magnet." Often I would step back and ask myself, *What is she talking about? Why is she saying these things?* You see, at that time my level of confidence was nowhere near Erieka's, and though I was accomplishing a lot of things, I didn't exactly see what she saw.

In the late nineties, life intervened, and I lost contact with Erieka. In 2006, now at another stage of my life, I began to reflect on the people who had had the most influence on me: people who had believed in, supported, and empowered me. I wanted to reconnect with those people; to include them in my inner circle. Erieka was at the top of my list, but I had no idea where she was or what she was doing, nor was I in contact with anyone who knew her. Instinctively, however, I knew she was still on her path – to get what was hers by divine right.

So I began an internet search for Erieka, starting first with her name. Nothing came up. Then I asked myself, *What was her path, her passion, her deepest desire?* I remembered that her passion was Africa. Her deepest desire was to work in Africa – to help the general public see the beauty of Africa and its people. She often said she wanted to be the companion or business associate of a high-level African dignitary or businessman. This would position her to truly make a difference in the lives of people living in Africa. It would also enable her to accomplish her own goals. Erieka was so entrenched in the African culture that she began dressing, exclusively, in the traditional dress of an African princess or queen. Her color was purple, symbolizing royalty. Even then, she had an awareness of global issues surrounding the African continent.

With this in mind, I resumed my internet search. This time, my search included words and phrases such as "consultants and advisors to Africa." Within minutes, several sites appeared with her name. My initial search revealed nothing because I was misspelling her name. Within days, I had reconnected with Erieka. After several e-mails and phone conversations, I learned that all of her dreams have come true. Yes, she has reached the power circles. She now resides in Ghana, where she has diplomatic status. She participates in the highest levels of the country's government and of the African Union. She walks among high-level dignitaries and influential people from all walks of life – not only in Africa but other countries as well.

How did she do it? She started with a strong intention and a belief. She also knew what success looked like to her. Then she got busy; she took action. Her eyes were already open wide; yet she opened them even wider to envision *all* of the possibilities God had in store for her – a life she truly believed was hers by divine right.

In an article appearing in the February 2007 issue of *Sister 2 Sister* magazine, one of Erieka's oldest and dearest friends of over 35 years shared a story of an island vacation they took together in the early seventies. According to the article, on the last night of their vacation, they decided to splurge. They located what looked liked the ritziest spot on the island – a restaurant at a resort hotel on the ocean that "dripped with elegance and reeked of money." Seated at a grand table with a view of the sea, Erieka, spreading her arms to encompass the room, announced, "I want all this – the diamonds, the rich clothing, never having to wonder if I can afford the cost of a meal in a place like this." Considering the fact that they were both young women of modest means and had careers that were not exactly on the big money track, her friend asked, "How do you think you'll get it? Erieka responded confidently, "I don't know. I just know I will. This is where I belong."

And get it she did. She has not just achieved success, but *optimum* success. She has reached great heights, but states, "I'm not finished yet."

If you ask the average person the key to success, you'll probable get many answers but the one you'll get most often is: hard work. Rarely, if ever, will you get this "Big Eyes" approach that the Eriekas of the world use. While working hard is important, hard work alone has never brought success. The world is filled with many hard-working people who are barely surviving. Others are even enjoying a certain degree of success, but it is highly unlikely they're experiencing optimum success.

What, then, is the key? I can't count the number of times I've been asked this question. There's no one key, nor is there a magic formula. But there is a recipe with the following ingredients:

- Clear intention

- Intense belief

- A positive self-image

- A large dose of confidence and self-esteem

- A clear vision

- Clear goals

- Focus

- Single-mindedness

- Nurturing relationships

- A positive attitude

- A healthy mind and body

- An attitude of abundance

- A giving spirit

The complete recipe is here. Combine of all these ingredients and you're guaranteed to achieve not just success, but *optimum* success.

Remember: We all have the capacity to achieve optimum success if only we will open our eyes wide, envision the possibilities, take action, and claim what is rightfully ours – what God has waiting for us.

An Invitation

Optimum success starts with an intention.
You must "intend" to be successful. You must make a
conscious, deliberate effort to be successful and have a
hunger and desire to have more, be more, and do more.

- Daisy Saunders

Achieving optimum success is an ongoing process. Along the way, there'll be many lessons learned. I hope you'll constantly review and revisit where you are and what success means to you.

As you've worked through this book, you've probably learned many lessons that you can apply to your life right now. You've probably also had a few "aha" experiences – moments of revelation or realization that opened your eyes and mind to the grand possibilities. What were some of yours? I'd love to hear about them.

Even if you read this book all the way through and didn't have one "aha" moment or learn a significant lesson, I invite you to e-mail me at **bigeyes@daisysaunders.com** with your comments and questions. I want to help you succeed at achieving your dreams! To that end, each month I will select from those of you who have emailed me two people to receive two free, no obligation, thirty-minute life-coaching sessions by phone.

You may also visit my website at **www.bigeyesintl.com** for recommended resources to help you open those big eyes even wider.

Use the notes fields that follow to record the lessons you've learned. Don't forget to review them frequently to help reinforce the messages, to encourage yourself, and to help keep you focused on your goals. So love your big eyes, open them wide, dream big, find your purpose, set your goals, and realize lasting and optimum success – in business and in life.

Remember: The only thing keeping you from experiencing and enjoying optimum success is *YOU*!

CHAPTER 1: EXAMINE YOUR PICTURE – Widen Your Eyes

Lessons Learned/Revelations:

_____

_____

_____

_____

_____

_____

_____

_____

_____

CHAPTER 2: ADJUST YOUR PICTURE – For Your Big Eyes Only

Lessons Learned/Revelations:

_____

_____

_____

_____

_____

_____

_____

_____

_____

_____

CHAPTER 3: HAVE A CLEAR VISION – See the Possibilities with Big Eyes

Lessons Learned/Revelations:

_____

_____

_____

_____

_____

_____

_____

_____

_____

_____

CHAPTER 4: SET GOALS – Keep Your Big Eyes Clear

Lessons Learned/Revelations:

_____

_____

_____

_____

_____

_____

_____

_____

_____

_____

CHAPTER 5: FOCUS – Keep Your Big Eyes on the Prize

Lessons Learned/Revelations:

_____

_____

_____

_____

_____

_____

_____

_____

_____

_____

CHAPTER 6: BUILD RELATIONSHIPS: Surround Yourself with Big-Eyed People

Lessons Learned/Revelations:

_____

_____

_____

_____

_____

_____

_____

_____

_____

_____

CHAPTER 7: BE POSITIVE – Keep Your Big Eyes Bright

Lessons Learned/Revelations:

_____

_____

_____

_____

_____

_____

_____

_____

_____

_____

CHAPTER 8: PRACTICE SELF-CARE - To Thine Own Big Eyes Be Good

Lessons Learned/Revelations:

_____

_____

_____

_____

_____

_____

_____

_____

_____

_____

CHAPTER 9: MIND YOUR MONEY – Open Your Big Eyes to Wealthfulness

Lessons Learned/Revelations:

_____

_____

_____

_____

_____

_____

_____

_____

_____

_____

CHAPTER 10: GIVE BACK – Shine Your Big Eyes on Others

Lessons Learned/Revelations:

_____

_____

_____

_____

_____

_____

_____

_____

_____

_____

USE THIS SPACE FOR ADDITIONAL NOTES, TO TRACK YOUR PROGRESS AND RECORD YOUR ACCOMPLISHMENTS *(Be sure to date your entries):*

_____

_____

_____

_____

_____

_____

_____

_____

_____

DAISY'S FAVORITES

James Allen, *As a Man Thinkest*, New York: G . P. Putnam's Sons, 1904.

Marc Allen, *Visionary Business*, California: New World Library, 1995.

Marc Allen and Mark Fisher, *How To Think Like a Millionaire*, California: New World Library, 1997.

Frank Armstrong III, *The Informed Investor*, New York: AMACON, 2004.

Claude Bristol and Harold Sherman, *TNT, The Power Within You*, New Jersey: Prentice Hall, 1954.

Eric Butterworth, *Spiritual Economics*, Missouri: Unity Books, 1993.

Byrne, Rhonda, *The Secret*, New York, ATRIA Books, 2006.

Dorothy Corkille Briggs, *Celebrate Your Self*, New York: Doubleday, 1977.

Viktor Frankl, *Man's Search for Meaning*, New York: Pocket Books, 1959.

Les Giblin, *How to Have Confidence and Power in Dealing with People*, New Jersey: Prentice-Hall, Inc., 1956.

Lynn Grabhorn, *Excuse Me, Your Life Is Waiting*, Virginia: Hampton Roads Publishing, 2000.

Hazrat Inayat Khan, *The Art of Being and Becoming*, New York: Omega Publications, (paperback) 1989.

Keith Harrell, *Attitude Is Everything, 10 Life Changing Steps to Turning Attitude Into Action*, New York: Harper Collins Publishers, 2000.

Jolley, Willie, *A Setback Is a Setup for a Comeback*, New York: St Martin's Press, 1999.

Dennis Kimbro and Napoleon Hill, *Think and Grow Rich...A Black Choice*, New York: Ballantine Books, 1991.

Robert T. Kiyosaki with Sharon L. Lechter, C.P.A., *Rich Dad Poor Dad*, New York: Warner Books, 2001.

Dr. Joseph Murphy, *The Power of Your Subconscious Mind*, New Jersey: Prentice Hall, 1963.

Joel Osteen, *Your Best Life Now*, New York: Warner Books, 2004.

Norman Vincent Peale, *The Power of Positive Thinking*, New York: Ballantine Books, 1952.

Rick Patino with Bill Reynolds, *Success is a Choice*, New York: Broadway Books, 1997.

Florence Scovel Shinn, *The Game of Life and How to Play It*, California: DeVorss & Company, 1925.

CONTACT INFORMATION

For information about Daisy Saunders'
workshops, seminars, keynotes, and published
materials, please visit her web site at:

www.**bigeyesintl**.com

or e-mail her at: **bigeyes@daisysaunders.com.**